Production 101

Raquel V. Benítez Rojas, BFTV, M.A., M.B.A.

Centennial College Press
Toronto

Centennial College Press
951 Carlaw Avenue
Toronto, Ontario M4K 3M2
https://centennialcollegepress.com/

Copyright © 2021 Raquel V. Benítez Rojas, BFTV, M.A., M.B.A.

All rights reserved. No part of this publication may be reproduced, distributed, or transmitted in any form or by any means, including photocopying, recording, or other electronic or mechanical methods, without the prior written permission of the publisher, except in the case of brief quotations embodied in critical reviews and certain other noncommercial uses permitted by copyright law. For permission requests, write to the publisher at the address above.

Copyeditor: Katie Martinuzzi

ISBN-13: 978-0-919852-78-5 (print)

Dedication

To my parents, Maria del Carmen Rojas Mateos and Francisco Benítez Gongora, for their constant support and trust.

To Carmen Llanos Acero for always being the person I could turn to in any life circumstance, for always being there.

To Comet, Sebastian and Sophie, you rock my world.

Contents

Introduction by Ramin Zahed ... 1

1. What is Copyright? ... 3
Introduction ... 3 – What is Copyright? ... 3 – Protecting a Copyright ... 4 – Assignment or Licensing of Copyright ... 5 – Who Owns the Copyright? ... 5 – Copyright and Moral Rights ... 6 – How Did We Arrive at the Protection of Intellectual Property Rights? ... 8 – What is an Audiovisual and Multimedia Work? ... 9 Fair Use ... 9 – Before Going into Production ... 10

2. Legal Organization ... 13
Introduction ... 13 – The Production Entity ... 14 – Steps to Creating a Corporation ... 14

3. Submission Forms ... 21
Introduction ... 21 – Submission Form #1 ... 22 – Submission Form #2 ... 24

4. Securing the Rights ... 27
Introduction ... 27 – Option, Purchase and Writing Agreements ... 27 – What are Guilds? ... 28 – Parts of an Option Agreement ... 28 – Option and Purchase Agreement Sample ... 30

5. Assignments ... 33
Introduction ... 33 – Assignment Agreement Provisions ... 34
Assignment and Waiver of Rights: Sample Agreement ... 35

6. Non-Disclosure and Non-Circumvention Agreements ... 43
Introduction ... 43 – Types of Non-Disclosure Agreements ... 43
Purposes of Non-Disclosure Agreements ... 44 – Non-Circumvention Agreements ... 44
Sample Agreements ... 44

7. In Search of the Money ... 63
Introduction ... 63 – The Bible ... 63 – The Teaser ... 64 – A Test ... 65 – Agreement for a Test Sample ... 66

8. Co-productions ... 69
Introduction ... 69 – International Co-productions ... 69
Basic Elements in any Co-production Agreement ... 71 – Some Key Aspects of Canadian Co-productions ... 71
Key Personnel ... 74 – Co-ventures ... 77 – Canadian Content ... 78 – Co-production Sample Agreement ... 80

9. Budget and Schedule ... 97
Budget ... 97 – Schedule ... 98

10. Insurance ... 101
Introduction ... 101 – Types of Insurance ... 101 – Errors and Omissions Insurance ... 102

11. Distribution ... 107
Introduction ... 107 – Distribution Agreements ... 108
International Standard Audiovisual Number (ISAN) ... 111

12. Rights Acquisition ... 143
Introduction ... 143 – Windows ... 143 – The Agreement ... 144

13. Merchandising ... 155
Introduction ... 155 – Tie-ins ... 155 – Basic Elements of a Merchandising License Agreement ... 156

Appendix I. The Berne Convention ... 159

Appendix II. Sample Production Budget ... 187
(a) Top Sheet ... 187 – Detauiled Budget CA $ ... 188

Appendix III. Sample Feature Schedule ... 190

Appendix IV. Sample Cue Sheet ... 191

Acknowledgements ... 192

About the Author ... 192

Introduction

Throughout the years, there have been numerous how-to books written by experts on how to bring your creative project from the page to the screen. The number of guides on producing entertainment content for the market can often be overwhelming. As the explosion of streaming content in recent years changes the media landscape, up-and-coming producers have more opportunities than ever before to roll up their sleeves and get to work as soon as inspiration strikes.

That's why this handy book by industry veteran Raquel Benitez Rojas is such a fantastic addition to the genre of how-to books dealing with live action and animated filmmaking. Raquel, who is a well-respected producer internationally, is the founder and president of Toronto-based Comet Entertainment Inc., a global company that offers advice on obtaining rights and producing properties for the worldwide market. She has over 35 years of experience in animation, production, licensing, and distribution, and knows the ins and outs of production and distribution in many territories around the globe.

What makes her take on the business different from others is her practical knowledge of the inner workings of the industry, because she herself has directed and produced content for TV, digital media, and theatrical releases. She reviews all the various steps of a project, from the earliest stages of development, through financing, clearing rights, hiring writers and artists, production, signing co-pro deals, and taking advantage of global tax credits, all the way to licensing, merchandising, distribution and residuals.

She has also taught the essentials of the production business to students in top colleges and universities around the world. That's why she knows how to package the material and present it to those who are just starting in the field or for those who are considering a career change or trying out new business models.

In short, I trust that Raquel will be the perfect guide to take you through the many stages of your animated or live action project. She spells out the necessary steps you need to take to navigate your way through the challenging stages of production. It's a journey worth taking, and this book will help you reach the fruition of your dreams with ease and confidence.

Ramin Zahed, Editor
Animation Magazine

Chapter 1
WHAT IS COPYRIGHT?

Introduction

You have an idea or have read a wonderful book that inspires you to produce a movie, or maybe you know someone whose story would make a great show. Fantastic! But before you jump up and down in happiness, there are many things you need to know. Developing ideas is not as simple as just coming up with the idea or concept and making it happen. You have to be sure you have followed the appropriate processes and have the necessary rights to be able to produce the project.

Basically, you need to obtain the **underlying rights** for your project. This means all licenses, permits, orders, and other agreements or permissions that allow the legal use of a creative property.

To turn that content into an audiovisual project requires that you hold the rights that have been transferred to you by the original creator, a process that is called **assignment of copyright**. In other words, producers need to obtain permission to use the copyrighted material.

There are many kinds of rights and ways to manage them, whether you are producing a movie, a TV series, arranging merchandising, or dealing with other media. Depending on the type of adaptation, you would obtain various rights. The process also depends partly on the nature of the underlying work, which might be a work "made for hire," an original work, an adaptation (of a book, for instance), and so on.

What is Copyright?

According to the Canadian Intellectual Property Office, **copyright** "is the exclusive legal right to produce, reproduce, publish, or perform an original literary, artistic, dramatic, or musical work."[1]

Copyright may apply to a broad range of original works, such as books, computer programs, drawings, paintings, sculptures, movies, songs, films, etc.

Copyright is usually explained using the metaphor of a "bundle of rights" to represent the different rights that are owned by a creator. There is also the analogy of a "bundle of sticks" or a "sand dune," in which each stick or tiny grain of sand represents one right. The copyright owner

1. Canadian Intellectual Property Office https://www.ic.gc.ca/eic/site/cipointernet-internetopic.nsf/eng/wr03719.html?Open&wt_src=cipo-cpyrght-main.

may be able to grant the different underlying rights to several third parties, enabling each of them to make different uses of the work.

The result is that a property can be simultaneously "owned" by multiple parties.

For a work to be protected by copyright, it must be **original**, originating with the author. You cannot copyright an idea, but you can copyright the physical form of the expression of an idea in order to protect it.

Copyright does not protect titles, ideas, concepts, names, slogans, processes, or information.

Protecting a Copyright

In the countries that are members of the **Berne Convention**, it is not a requirement to register a work for copyright protection. The Berne Convention established the basics of how we understand copyright today. It was initially signed in Berne, Switzerland, on September 9, 1886, completed in Paris on May 4, 1896, and revised in Berlin on November 13, 1914, Rome on June 26, 1928, Brussels on June 26, 1948, Stockholm on July 14, 1967, and Paris on July 24, 1971. It was later amended on September 28, 1979. (Please refer to Appendix 1.)[2]

The agreement states that if a work is under copyright in one of the signatory countries, then this copyright is valid in all countries that are members and signatories of the Berne Convention.[3] At present, there are 176 signatory countries (out of the 195 countries in the world today).

While the **registration** of a copyright at an intellectual property office is not required in order to validate or protect the copyright, registration serves two purposes. First, it aids in the protection of the copyright as it can serve as useful evidence in a dispute requiring legal proof of ownership of copyright. Secondly, it makes others aware of the copyright claim. In Canada, copyrights are registered at CIPO (Canadian Intellectual Property Office).

If a dispute about ownership of copyright arises, the person claiming the copyright must be able to prove that he or she is the rightful owner.

Creators can also obtain proof of ownership by registered mail through what a process that is called "registration of the poor," wherein the author sends themselves a copy of their work in a sealed, certified self-addressed envelope. This also helps to establish when the work was created. This procedure is widely accepted in countries that are members of the Berne Convention.

Use of a copyright notice raises public awareness, both of the copyright claim and of the copyright owner. The notice contains the word "copyright" and/or the copyright symbol, ©.

2. https://global.oup.com/booksites/content/9780198259466/15550001 (last accessed December 6, 2019).
3. Berne Convention of Literary and Artistic Works, List of Berne Convention signatories (https://copyright-house.co.uk/copyright/countries-berne-convention.htm).

The symbol must be followed by the date and name of the author, and it should be visible in all media.

For example:

Copyright © 2021 Raquel Benitez Rojas. All rights reserved.

The length of time a copyright remains valid varies depending on the country, with each having its own specific copyright law.

In Canada, copyright currently exists for the lifetime of the author plus another 50 years following the end of the year of their death, although this will be changed to 70 years no later than the end of 2022 under the terms of the revised free trade agreement between Canada, the United States, and Mexico. The same length of time (50 years) is used for cable programs and broadcasts, starting from the year in which the broadcast was made.

In the typographical field, copyright lasts for 25 years from the publishing date.[4]

Assignment or Licensing of Copyright

The copyright owner can assign or **license** the rights to another person or entity, in order to authorize the performance of the work(s).

For copyright owners, it is always recommended that they be a member of a recognized **collective management society**, such as SOCAN (Society of Composers, Authors and Music Publishers of Canada), SGAE (Sociedad General de Autores y Editores), SIAE (Società Italiana degli Autori ed Editori), ALCS (Authors' Licensing and Collecting Society), ASCAP (American Society of Composers, Authors, and Publishers), etc. They assist in the licensing of rights and the collection of royalties. These societies will act on behalf of their members (authors) to negotiate licenses with third parties who would like to use the protected works.

Who Owns the Copyright?

Normally, the owner of the copyright is the author or the creator. If the work is created during the course of employment, the employer owns the copyright, unless the author has entered into a written agreement with their employer, permitting them to retain some rights to use the work.

When you are a freelance writer who has been hired to create a script, the ownership of the work should be specified in the agreement. Ownership of copyright can be transferred or assigned by contract.

---

4. About Copyright and Related Rights (JIPO) (https://www.jipo.gov.jm/node/47).

Depending on what is agreed between the parties, a license for the use of rights may last for the entire duration of the copyright or for a specific time period.

Copyright and Moral Rights

There are two kinds of rights included within copyright:

(1) **Economic rights**, which allow the owner of the rights to obtain financial compensation from the use of their work by third parties. Based on this, the rights owner of a work can obtain benefits from:

- The reproduction of the work in various forms,
- Its public performance,
- Its recording,
- Its translation into other languages, and/or
- Its adaptation.

(2) The **non-economic interests** of the author, which are called **moral rights**. Moral rights (or *droits moraux*) are perpetual (with exceptions in some countries, as noted below), inalienable and imprescriptible.

- Perpetual: these rights survive after the death of the author, even including when the author's work is in the public domain.
- Inalienable: this means that these rights cannot be bought and may not be transferred in any way.
- Imprescriptible: this means that the author cannot lose his or her moral rights by not having exercised them for a period of time; furthermore these rights cannot be obtained through extended usage.

Moral rights are generally composed of four items:[5]

- The **right of divulgation**, which gives the author the right to decide when his or her work may be shown to the world;
- The **right of withdrawal or disavowal**, which allows the creator, who has transferred part or all of his or her rights, to prevent the transferee from exercising the rights granted in exchange for financial compensation;
- The **right of attribution**, which allows the author to be recognized as the creator of a work;
- The **right of integrity**, which allows the author to avoid the distortion of the work without the moral rights owner's authorization.

---

5. Raymond Sarraute, "Current Theory on the Moral Right of Authors and Artists under French Law," *The American Journal of Comparative Law* 16, no. 4 (1968): 465–86. Accessed January 11, 2020. doi:10.2307/838764.

Moral rights are often a characteristic of countries which possess a **civil law** structure, a legal system originating in Europe and based on Roman law whose principles are structured into a codified, referable system. Moral rights are not as well established in **common law** countries, where legal principles have been derived from, and are largely based on, the decisions of courts. Moral rights are always tied to individuals—never to companies or corporations—and are inalienable, perpetual (with some exceptions), and exempt from prescription. In many common law countries, you are able to waive your moral rights, but never to transfer them contractually. The province of Quebec uses a civil law system. The other provinces use common law. However, moral rights are recognized in section 14.1 of the Copyright Act of Canada.

In Canada, a legal judgment issued in 1982 in the case of Snow vs. Eaton Centre Ltd. (1982), 70 CPR (2d) 105, recognized moral rights as being an integral part of an artistic work and protectable by the artist. The Eaton Centre, a large shopping center in downtown Toronto, was found liable for violating Michael Snow's moral rights when they decorated his sculpture of flying geese, entitled "Flight Stop," with some red Christmas bows. Michael Snow complained that this was a distortion, mutilation, or modification of his artistic work and was detrimental to his reputation. His lawyer compared it to dangling earrings from the Venus de Milo. The judge agreed that Mr. Snow's moral rights had been violated and ordered the Eaton Centre to remove the bows.

Moral rights were included in the Berne Convention in 1928 and were first recognized in France and Germany. Moral rights are specifically protected under the Copyright Act in Canada. The length of protection varies depending on the type of work to which the rights are attached. Under the Act, a work's moral rights are protected for the same period of time as the work's copyright.

In the United States, moral rights are recognized under the Visual Artists Rights Act of 1990 (VARA). The act sets out how and to which areas they apply within the visual arts.

Each country has its own limitations on these rights, and you must review those limitations before asking for an assignment or waiver of rights. For example, in Denmark, moral rights last for the duration of the life of the author plus 70 years; in France, they are perpetual; and in Canada and the United States, they can be waived.

How Did We Arrive at the Protection of Intellectual Property Rights?

Let us talk a little about history.

The first reference that we have to intellectual property protection takes us back to 500 B.C.E. At that time, in Sybaris, a Greek colony, chefs were granted year-long monopolies for creating specific dishes.

In Roman times, in the first century C.E., there is a fascinating case of plagiarism or literary piracy where Fidentinus, without citing the source, was caught reciting the works of Martial, although there is no known Roman law protecting intellectual property.

In later days, in the Florentine Republic, we start to see more recognition of what we understand today as intellectual property. At that time, royal favours granted exclusivity and ownership surrounding the rights to intellectual works.

Three lines of thought will lead us to the current system of intellectual property rights and the reasons we have it:

The Utilitarian Theory

Advocated by many philosophers, among which Jeremy Bentham (1748–1832) and John Stuart Mill (1806–1873) are the most notable, this theory argued that by having intellectual property rights, we would have a better society. The country that follows this theory and represents these values is the United States, which includes intellectual property rights protection in its Constitution. Article 1, section 8, clause 8 reads: "Patent and Copyright Clause of the Constitution. [Congress shall have the power] To promote the progress of science and useful arts, by securing for limited times to authors and inventors the exclusive right to their respective writings and discoveries."[6]

Natural Rights Theory

Represented by the English philosopher and physician John Locke (1632–1704), this theory claims that it is simply a natural right to claim the ownership rights to something you have created. The country that best represents this way of thinking is France.

Personhood Theory

Originated by the German philosopher Georg Wilhelm Friedrich Hegel (1770–1831), with

---

6. W. Spivey et al., "Implications of the America Invents Act for R&D Managers: Connecting the Patent Life Cycle with the Technology Development Process," *Research Technology Management* 57, no. 5 (2014): 43.

professor Margaret Jane (Peggy) Radin (1941) as its leading proponent, this theory claims that, for an individual to achieve his or her full artistic potential, he or she must have control over all the parts of his/her body and the intellectual property that is part of his/her "personhood." This theory has been implemented together with the natural rights theory in many countries around the world.

What is an Audiovisual and Multimedia Work?

Audiovisual works are to be understood as described by the AVMS, the Audiovisual and Multimedia Section of the IFLA, the International Federation of Library Associations and Institutions, in their study *Guidelines for Audiovisual and Multimedia Collection Management in Libraries* as:[7]

(i) visual recordings (with or without a soundtrack) irrespective of their physical base and recording process used, which are:

(a) intended for public reception either by television or by means of projection on screens or by any other means.

(b) intended to be made available to the public.

(ii) sound recordings irrespective of their physical base and the recording process used, which are:

(a) intended for public reception by means of broadcasting or any other means.

(b) intended to be made available to the public.

Multimedia works are to be understood as a combination of two or more digital media used in a computer application or data file. Multimedia applications are often interactive, synonymous in this sense with digital media.

In a more general sense, any program, presentation, or computer application in which two or more communication media are used simultaneously or in close association could be considered a multimedia application.[7]

Note that **still images** accompanying text are considered illustrations. By still images, we refer to photos or pictures by an artist.

Fair Use

In some countries, i.e., the USA, the use of protected works does not infringe on the copyright owner's rights in certain instances. These cases include, but are not limited to, commentary, criticism, education, news, parody, private study, reporting, research, review, satire, scholarship,

7. Guidelines for Audiovisual and Multimedia Collection Management in Libraries: https://www.ifla.org/files/assets/avms/publications/ifla_avms_guidelines_revision_final_draft_april_2017_for_publication_00000002.pdf.

search engines, and teaching. This is called **fair use**. In Canada and some other countries, there is a similar, but not identical, concept called **fair dealing**. There are some elements that are key to this use:

- **The purpose.** What is the intended use of the copyrighted material? Is it for education, research, or commercial purposes?
- **The character.** What do we want to do with the work? Is it an ongoing use or isolated? Is it being distributed and how?
- **The amount.** What percentage of the copyrighted work have we used? Is it just some small excerpts or a large piece?
- **The alternatives.** Was it necessary to use this work or could we have used another work?
- **The nature.** Was its use of public interest, and was it previously used by others? What is the status of the work? Is it published or unpublished?
- **The effect.** Does the use compete with the sales of the original work?

Before Going into Production

Before going into production, you should ask: What rights must I have, and what are the procedures that I must follow, as a producer, to obtain the underlying rights needed for my production?

(1) **Obtaining the underlying rights.** As previously explained, you do need to hold the necessary rights for the product you are creating. This does not imply that you must have the right to everything.

(2) **A copyright report on the underlying works must be obtained.** This is what we call **chain of title**, where we ensure that we have a complete report on who has been the owner of the copyright in each particular step of the process.

(3) **The basics of the work (an idea, a sequence of events, and characters) should be confirmed.** If the production is going to be based on a book, for example, you will need to obtain the rights to the book for your purpose.

(4) **A title report must be obtained prior to the final title selection.** Through a rights company, you have to research the title of your work to be sure it is not already in use by someone else

(5) **Written releases have to be obtained from any recognizable living persons.** If you are portraying someone, or someone is shown in the screen production, you must obtain the proper release forms in order to depict them on screen.

(6) **The producer must obtain the right to edit, modify, add to, and/or delete material.**

This is very important. As a producer, you might have the rights to a book, but you might want to tell the story in a different way in your screen production. You must have written authorization from the book's writer to alter or modify his/her work, to add characters, remove them, etc., based on the needs of your production.

(7) **To use of pre-existing or original music, the producer has to obtain all necessary performance, synchronization, and recordings rights.** The music must be in the public domain, or if you are hiring someone or using music from a creative source, you must obtain all the necessary rights to use it in the screen production.

(8) **All the agreements must be confirmed in a written agreement, signed by the producer and each relevant individual.**

(9) **Written releases must be secured if distinctive locations are being recorded.** If, for example, you are recording at the CN Tower in downtown Toronto, you must obtain the necessary permissions and releases to record there and to use its image.

(10) **In the case of actual events, the producer must confirm that the author's sources are independent,** i.e., newspapers, magazines, interviews, etc. and not from another author's work.

(11) **Right of publicity (also called personality rights).** In the USA, this is a recognized right that every person has in order to control the commercial use of unequivocal aspects of their identity. This implies that you must obtain the necessary clearances to use this person's identity. Living persons and even the deceased may have a **right of publicity**, so you have to determine if such rights exist and obtain the necessary authorizations or clearances.

Chapter 2
LEGAL ORGANIZATION

Introduction

Undertaking production is a big step. There are many aspects that you have to take into consideration before you begin your production, and one of them is the legal form under which you will operate your business.

Normally, a producer is advised to set up a **corporation**. The primary reason behind this is to limit his/her liability, but it is often also necessary because incorporation is an essential requirement for most of the tax credits available, as well as for investors, banks, etc.

You can open a single-purpose company for that particular production where the exclusive activity of this corporation is the production of this particular project, and use the name of the project as the name of this new corporation. It may also be advisable to set up your own production company to operate your production business and serve as the parent company for your single-purpose production companies. The parent company will then be the sole owner of the single-purpose production company.

If the production is a co-production by two or more entities that have come together to complete the project, or a group of related projects, they may enter into a **joint venture arrangement**. This type of arrangement could be structured through a joint venture agreement between the entities, or by incorporating a single-purpose corporation for the co-production in which the entities who are the co-producers each own a proportionate number of the corporation's shares. In that situation, your production company will hold a number of the shares of the corporation set up to undertake the co-production that is proportionate to your interest in the co-production.

Do not worry if you do not want to use the name of the production as the corporate name. When you file your articles of incorporation, you can apply to incorporate a numbered company. The government will assign a corporation number to the new corporation, which will be combined with the name of the jurisdiction in which you are incorporating and an abbreviation such as "Inc.," "Ltd.," or "Corp." to create the name of the corporation. For example, if the assigned corporation number is 9876543, you have selected the abbreviation "Inc.," and you are incorporating under the laws of Ontario, the corporation's name will be 9876543 Ontario Inc. The steps to incorporate and organize the corporation are laid out later in this chapter.

The Production Entity

As I already explained, producers generally form a production company. A production company can be any form of business entity, such as a corporation, a limited partnership ("LP"), or, in the United States, a limited liability company ("LLC"). In Canada, in most circumstances, corporations are used as production entities. The reason for that is that they have the following four characteristics:

- Flexibility in terms of the tax treatment or pass-through tax treatment (this is for US-based companies as they do not have to pay federal income tax);
- Flexibility in the allocation of power among and between shareholders (i.e., the owners of the corporation);
- Ability to provide the benefits of limited liability for the business owners; and
- Greater flexibility in deciding how to split their financial interests.

A corporation usually provides more flexibility than a partnership and also provides protection against personal liability. **Limited partnerships** offer limited partners some protection against personal liability, but they are complex and used much less often than corporations. If you are considering entering into a partnership arrangement, you should consult an experienced lawyer because these arrangements can be quite complicated. The balance of this chapter will discuss the use of a corporation as your production entity.

The owners of a corporation are known as **shareholders**. The proportion of shares each of them holds will generally determine how much control they will have over the operations of the corporation. If there is more than one shareholder, it is imperative to have all of the shareholders enter into a **shareholders' agreement**. This is discussed in more detail later in this chapter.

Shareholders are protected from personal responsibility for the debts of the corporation, so their risk in the business is limited to the amount of money they originally invested. However, if they give personal guarantees (which may be required by banks or other lenders in some circumstances), they will be personally liable for the guaranteed amount.

Steps to Creating a Corporation

1. Corporate Jurisdiction

In Canada, there are two ways to incorporate your business: under federal jurisdiction or in one of the 13 provincial and territorial jurisdictions.

There are some differences and benefits associated with each option. In Canada, federal corporations are incorporated under the Canada Business Corporations Act ("CBCA") and can carry out business anywhere in Canada. They can use their registered corporate name in all provinces and territories, subject to complying with extra-provincial registration in each province or territory where they develop their activities.

The rules for provincially registered corporations are based on the legislation of the province or territory where they are incorporated and they can only carry on business there. If the corporation wants to expand its business or would like to open an office in another province or territory, it must file for registration in the new province to do business in that province or territory. It is important to note that provincial incorporation provides corporate name protection only within the place of its incorporation, so it is necessary to obtain a name clearance as part of the extra-provincial registration process in each province or territory where your corporation intends to do business. If your corporation's name is too similar to the name of a corporation that is already registered in that jurisdiction, your application for registration may be denied unless you change your corporation's name.

Another consideration is the cost of incorporating. Federal corporations are incorporated at the federal level and then in one or more provinces where the corporation intends to carry out their activities. Therefore if you only intend to do business through the corporation in one province or territory, the cost of incorporation may be higher for federal incorporation. There are two provinces, Ontario and Prince Edward Island, where federal corporations do not have to pay extra filling fees if the company is federally incorporated.

To summarize, it is essential to decide where to incorporate, taking into account whether you will be carrying out business in one province or territory or throughout Canada, and whether it is essential to be able to use the corporation's name in multiple jurisdictions.

2. Corporate Name

This looks like the fun part, maybe even the easy bit, but trust me, it is not that simple. In theory, each jurisdiction has its own guidelines and requirements for corporate names, and there are no mandatory requirements for choosing a name. Remember if you do not have a name you will be assigned a number, which is that of the registration of the company.

As we have seen previously, a federally incorporated corporation is entitled to use its corporate name in all Canadian jurisdictions, so some restrictions apply. The CBCA requires that all proposed names be distinctive. To achieve this, the name must include a unique element and should usually also include descriptive elements, although that is not required. The distinctive element could be a coined (made-up) word or an acronym. In the case of my company, Comet Entertainment Inc., we have a name and a word that describes the activity of my corporation. "Inc." is the legal ending. The legal ending, which may be "Inc.," "Corp.," "Ltd.," or the French equivalent or long form of those names, indicates that the entity is a corporation. The names of all for-profit corporations must have a legal ending. Not-for-profit corporations may not use any of those legal endings and are not required to have a legal ending except when a numbered corporation is being incorporated. In that case, other legal endings such as "Association," "Society," "Centre," or "Institute," or the French variant of one of those names, must be used. The name cannot be the same as, or confusingly similar to, the name of another corporation, or organization, or a registered trademark. It also cannot be misleading or confusing as to who owns the business. As well, there are some prohibitions on using certain words as part of the name. If the corporation intends to operate in Quebec, a French form of the name should be selected at the time of incorporation.

Instead of selecting a corporate name, as noted above, the owners can apply to incorporate a numbered corporation. In that case, the name will consist of the registration number assigned by the government, the name of the jurisdiction, and a legal ending (e.g., 01234567 Alberta Inc.). Numbered company names are normally used for sole-purpose corporations like the ones used in media or when the corporation will operate the business under another registered business name. If there is an urgent need to get a corporation incorporated immediately, a numbered corporation can be used to avoid the delays that may be involved in trying to decide on a suitable corporate name.

Unless a numbered corporation is being incorporated, the proposed corporate name must be searched using the Newly Upgraded Automated Name Search ("NUANS®") system or, for Quebec incorporations, the Centre Informatique du Registre des Entreprises du Québec ("CIDREQ") system. Once the name has been searched and reserved, the NUANS search report must be submitted to the government with the Articles of Incorporation. Approval of the corporation's name must be obtained for federal incorporations. Ontario requires a NUANS name search report but leaves it to the incorporator to determine whether the name meets the requirements of the Business Corporations Act (Ontario) and its regulations regarding corporate names. If the name you have chosen does not meet those requirements, you could be required to change it at a later date if your corporate name is challenged.

3. Articles of Incorporation

Corporations must file **articles of incorporation** with the appropriate government agencies.

The incorporator should obtain legal and tax advice before completing the articles of incorporation. Setting your corporation up properly is extremely important. It can be very costly if it is not done correctly initially, and you have to fix it later. The articles of incorporation must set out the corporation's name, the location of the registered office, the number of directors to be elected or the minimum and maximum number of directors that the corporation may have, the names and addresses of the corporation's first directors, the classes of shares and any limits on the number of shares that may be issued to each class (the "authorized capital"), and what approvals are required for the transfer of the corporation's shares. For-profit corporations do not have to identify the corporation's business activity in the articles, but if there are to be restrictions on its business activities (which is rare in Canada), those must be identified.

Once the articles of incorporation have been prepared, they are filed electronically with the appropriate government agency. The government agency then issues a **certificate of incorporation**, which identifies the incorporation date and assigns a unique corporation number to the corporation.

4. Organization of the Corporation

Once the certificate of incorporation has been issued, the corporation will need to be organized. As mentioned earlier, corporations are owned by shareholders. If there is a single shareholder, that person or corporation will own 100 percent of the shares. Any number of shares can be issued; it is the percentage of ownership that is important. If there is more than one shareholder, the incorporators will have to determine what percentage of the shares each of the shareholders will own. There can also be different types (referred to as "classes") of shares issued. For example, shareholders who are participating as investors but will not be actively involved in the production may receive non-voting shares with rights to preferential dividends, while the shareholders who will be actively involved will hold the voting shares. The voting shareholders elect the **directors** who form the board of directors. The directors are responsible for managing the corporation. The directors appoint **officers**, such as the president, secretary, treasurer, etc.

All corporations are required to keep certain records by law, including:
- Articles of incorporation and any amendments;
- Corporation by-laws;
- Minutes of the meetings of the shareholder(s);
- Shareholder agreements and resolutions;
- Minutes of the meetings of the directors and their resolutions;
- Directors, officers, and securities register;
- Share transfer register; and
- All documents filed with any government agency.

All of these documents are kept together in a corporate minute book. The corporation also needs to have a corporate seal, which is used in legal documents.

After the corporation has been created, the corporation needs to be organized. The initial organization is achieved by meetings of the directors and shareholders. Alternatively, the directors and shareholders can pass resolutions by signature.

The organization must carry out the following steps:
- Approval of corporate by-laws (by the directors and shareholders);
- Allocation of shares to shareholders (by the directors);
- Election of directors (by the shareholders);
- Appointment of corporate officers (by the directors);
- Passage of other organizational resolutions; and
- Filing of an initial information return with the government of the incorporating jurisdiction.

Once you have completed the organization of the corporation, you can open your bank account. To do so, a copy of the articles of incorporation and a list of the directors and officers will need to pass the specific form of banking resolution required by your bank, designating the directors and officers who are authorized to sign bank documents.

If there is more than one shareholder, it is very important for them to enter into a **shareholders' agreement**. A shareholders' agreement establishes the rules that govern the operations of the corporation. It is a very flexible form of business agreement. Without a shareholders' agreement, the majority shareholder or group of shareholders will have the right to elect the board of directors and make most of the business decisions. To protect minority shareholders, a shareholders' agreement will set out who will be the directors and officers or how they will be elected or appointed, and how many and to whom shares in the corporation may be issued. Usually, it will also identify types of decisions that require unanimous consent or the consent of a high proportion of the shareholders. Some examples of these types of decisions might include the sale or termination of the production, the distribution of shares to other persons, such as other producers or investors (which potentially dilutes the holdings of the existing shareholders), or the undertaking of new projects. Most importantly, it should specify the procedures to be followed if the shareholders wish to go their separate ways. A split between shareholders is much like a divorce. It can be bitter, as well as being very messy and expensive to negotiate if the shareholders have not agreed in advance on a process to deal with this situation. If more than one shareholder is going to be involved, it is essential to negotiate a comprehensive shareholders' agreement at the time you incorporate your corporation; I cannot stress this enough.

4. Permits and Licenses

There are still some legal requirements to meet after setting up the corporation; these are:
- Registering with the Canada Revenue Agency (CRA) for a **federal business number** (for all corporations). This identification number is used for any operations related to the government, such as federal corporate income taxes, import/export account, GST/HST, and payroll;
- If you use non-corporate business names, other than the one registered, registering them;
- If needed, registration for a provincial sales tax account;
- Setting up Employer Health Tax and Workers' Compensation accounts; and
- Obtaining provincial and/or municipal licenses as needed.

5. Other Considerations

A corporation is a separate legal entity from its shareholders, directors, and officers, and it must have its own financial statements, file its own tax returns, and satisfy any legal obligations. There are tax consequences to how funds are put into the corporation (for example as the subscription price for shares or as a loan) and how funds are paid out of the corporation (for example as dividends to the shareholders, loan repayments, payments of salaries or expenses, etc.). The corporation's funds must not be confused or mingled with the funds of the shareholders and maintaining proper accounting records of all transactions is essential.

Although shareholders of corporations are usually shielded from personal liability for the corporation's debts, directors and officers of corporations may be held personally liable if a corporation fails to fulfill its legal responsibilities, or if they act negligently or commit willful misconduct. Many of these types of personal liabilities are imposed by statutes (acts) passed by the federal, provincial, or territorial government. For example, if a corporation fails to remit to the CRA the source deductions—income tax, Canadian Pension Plan (CPP) contributions, and Employment Insurance (EI) premiums—that it is required to deduct from its employees' salaries, the directors may be personally liable. In some circumstances, directors may be liable for the corporation's failure to pay income tax or to remit Harmonized Sales Tax (HST)/Goods and Services Tax (GST). In an insolvency situation, directors may be liable for up to six months' wages of the corporation's employees. Liability may also arise out of occupational health and safety or environmental violations. If you become a director or officer of a corporation, you must take your responsibilities very seriously and closely monitor the corporation's activities and financial status.

You should also insist that the corporation purchase directors' and officers' liability insurance. While it will not cover all potential liabilities, it may provide coverage for the legal costs of defending a claim against the directors and officers, and, in the case of negligence, it should cover any awards for damages. In the case of the wilful misconduct of a director or officer, it should protect the directors and officers who are innocent and did not condone the misconduct.

The best advice is to consult with qualified professionals (lawyer, accountant/tax advisor, insurance broker) when you decide to incorporate and get proper advice about how to set up and operate the corporation. Taking the initiative, in the beginning, to get your business set up properly is well worth the time, effort, and cost.

Chapter 3
SUBMISSION FORMS

Introduction

When a creator wants to develop his/her ideas, book(s), outline(s), etc. into some sort of audio-visual production, it seems evident that they will seek out the relevant professionals who can make that possible. It is also understandable that they will reach out to a producer or a production company. You might think this seems simple: just a matter of preparing a nice presentation and sending it to the producer. Well, you are WRONG!

If you are a creator, it is not only necessary that you have some sort of copyright protection for your work, but also that you follow the rules of the game. Usually, producers or production companies receive a large number of proposals to develop. This does not mean that they will develop all of them, or that they might not already have a similar idea to yours or have read a third-party proposal which is like yours.

So, what do you do?

(1) Before sending any material to anyone, you have to take the steps needed to protect your copyright, as we have seen in the first chapter of this book.

(2) Be sure to investigate the company to which you would like to submit your material, to be sure that they are looking for that kind of outline and that they are the right partner to produce it, i.e., do not send an animation series proposal to a news broadcaster.

(3) Check on their website to determine whether they have some kind of submission protocol; usually, they do.

(4) Follow their protocol. Most serious companies have what they call a **submission form**, which is a form that you have to fill out before sending any materials to anyone. You will find some examples below. These forms aim to protect the parties, primarily the producer, from future litigation over the copyright of a property. Basically, producers do not want to receive any unsolicited material.

Submission Form # 1

Title [of the Work Being Submitted]:

To whom it may concern,

I am submitting, for your consideration, the referenced material entitled _____ (hereinafter referred to as the "submitted material") pursuant to the following terms and conditions, in furtherance of the prospect of producing this particular content.

1. I represent and warrant that I am the submitted material's author; that I am the sole owner of the right and title to the submitted material; that I have the authority to make this submission and to grant the rights that will be conveyed to you if we agree to proceed with a production, and that the submitted material does not infringe upon a third party's copyright. I agree to hold you harmless from any claims, losses, judgments, and expenses (including reasonable legal fees and costs) that are incurred by you due to my breach of the aforementioned warranties and/or any other provision of this Submission and Release.

2. I understand that you create material in-house and, as such, that you may be developing a concept that is similar to the material that I am submitting to you. Furthermore, I am also aware that a third party may submit material to you that is comparable to mine, which you may decide to acquire and produce. You may produce said material, without any obligation to me of any kind, utilizing a concept that, although similar to the submitted material, was independently created by a third party or you.

3. I am interested in having you evaluate my submitted material. I know that because of your stature in the industry, you receive many screenplays, treatments, ideas, stories, formats, and suggestions for content to produce. As a consequence thereof, I understand that you cannot read, accept, and evaluate the submitted material unless I sign and return this Submission Release.

4. I acknowledge that no confidential relationship now exists or will ever exist between us by reason of this agreement or submission of the submitted material to you. No implied agreements will exist between us as a consequence of this unsolicited submission or conversations in reference thereto.

5. I agree that any portion of the submitted material that may be freely used by the public because it is not protected under copyright law or is in the public domain may be utilized by you. The submitted material which you are free to use without any obligation to me shall be referred to as "unprotected material" henceforth. If all or any part of said submitted material is not unprotected material because it is protected under copyright law, then it shall be referred to herein as "protected material."

6. I have retained an original copy of the submitted material which is being submitted for your assessment. I fully release your company from any and all liabilities in connection with loss, damage, or failure to return said submitted material.

7. I hereby state that I have read and understood this agreement and that no oral representations of any kind have been made to me and that this agreement states our entire understanding with reference to the subject matter hereof. Any modification or waiver of any of the provisions of this agreement must be in writing and signed by both of us.

8. In the event of any dispute, claim, question, or difference arising out of, or relating to, this Agreement or the breach thereof, the parties shall use their best endeavors to settle such disputes, claims, questions, or differences. To this effect, they shall consult and negotiate with each other, in good faith and understanding of their mutual interests, to reach a just and equitable solution satisfactory to all parties promptly upon notice by any party specifying full particulars of the dispute and, if they do not reach such solution within thirty (30) days thereafter, then either party may deliver written notice to the other party requiring resolution, by judicial process, and thereafter refer the dispute, claim, question, or difference in issue to the Courts of the Province of _____, Canada or, if within its exclusive jurisdiction, the Federal Court of Canada, and the decisions of such Courts shall be binding on both parties.

This submission and release given by:

Name: _____

Address: _____

Telephone: _____

E-mail: _____

Concerning the material entitled: _____

Submitted to: _____ (department) _____

Place and Date: _____

Submission Form #2

To the CEO of _____.

Dear Sir/Madam,

I desire to submit to you for your consideration the following described material (herein called "Submitted Material") written, composed, owned or controlled by me and intended to be used by you as the basis for one or more theatrical motion pictures:

_____

I recognize the possibility that the Submitted Material may be identical with, or similar to, material which has, or may come to you from other sources. Such similarity in the past has given rise to litigation such that, unless you can obtain adequate protection in advance, you will refuse to consider the Submitted Material. The protection for you must be sufficiently broad to protect you, your related corporations, and your and their employees, agents, licensees, and assigns, and all parties to whom you submit material. Therefore, all references to you include each and all of the foregoing.

As a material inducement to you to examine and consider the Submitted Material, and in consideration of your so doing, I represent, warrant, and agree to the following terms and conditions:

1. I acknowledge that the Submitted Material is submitted by me voluntarily, on an unsolicited basis, and not in confidence, and that no confidential relationship is intended or created between us by reason of the submission of the Submitted Material. Nothing in this agreement, including the submission of the Submitted Material, shall be deemed to place you in any different position from any other member of the public with respect to the Submitted Material. Accordingly, you may use any part of the Submitted Material, which could freely be used by any member of the public, without liability to me.

2. You agree that you shall not use the Submitted Material unless you shall first negotiate with me and agree upon compensation to be paid to me for such use, but I understand and agree that your use of material containing features or elements similar to or identical with those contained in the Submitted Material shall not obligate you to negotiate with me or entitle me to any compensation if you determine that you have an independent legal right to use such other material which is not derived from me (either because such features or elements were not new or novel, or were not originated by me, or were or may hereafter be independently created and submitted by other persons, including your employees).

3. I represent and warrant that I own individually or together with those other persons

executing this agreement, the Submitted Material, that the Submitted Material is free of all claims or encumbrances, and that I have the exclusive right to offer all rights in the Submitted Material to you.

4. I agree that no obligation of any kind is assumed or may be implied against you by reason of your consideration of the Submitted Material or any discussions or negotiations we may have with respect thereto, except pursuant to an express written agreement hereafter executed by you and me which, by its terms, will be the only contract between us.

5. Any claim, controversy or dispute arising hereunder shall be settled by arbitration before a single arbitrator in accordance with the rules of the Ontario Film and Development Corporation located in Toronto, Ontario. The award of the arbitrator shall be binding upon the parties and judgment there may be entered in any court. The prevailing party shall be entitled to all arbitration costs, and reasonable attorneys' fees.

6. I have retained a copy of the Submitted Material. I assume full responsibility for any loss of the Submitted Material, irrespective or whether it is lost, stolen, or destroyed in transit, or while in your possession, or otherwise.

7. Except as otherwise provided in this agreement, I hereby release you of and from any and all claims demands and liabilities of every kind whatsoever, known or unknown, that may arise in relation to the Submitted Material or by reason of any claim now or hereafter made by me that you have used or appropriated the Submitted Material, except for fraud or willful injury on your part.

8. No statements or representations have been made except those expressly stated in this agreement. This agreement may be modified only by subsequent written agreement signed both by you and me.

Very Truly Yours,

Writer _____

Address _____

_____

Phone/Email _____

Date _____

Encl: Submitted Material as Described Above

Signed _____

Chapter 4
SECURING THE RIGHTS

Introduction

As we have seen before, the producer needs to acquire all the necessary rights in the property that he or she wants to develop, including the right to exploit the property that will allow the distribution and sale of the final product.

In this chapter, we will discuss all the agreements that are necessary for either an author or a producer to produce a show. We will talk about the chain of title, which is the transfer of title to a property, assignments, compliances, submissions, rights clearances, and, generally speaking, all documents that must be executed to avoid future litigation.

The chain of title involves any and all rights agreements between the rightsholders and the party who wants to buy the rights, and any other related documents that are needed.

As a producer, you have to confirm who owns the rights. This requires a copyright search.

Option, Purchase and Writing Agreements

There are generally two forms of rights agreements:

(1) **Option/purchase agreement**: when you are acquiring the work "as is"; and

(2) **Writing agreement**: when you are commissioning the creation of a work.

Unless you are optioning a script, normally these will require two separate agreements, which are entered into with different individuals.

An **option** is an arrangement, usually exclusive and lasting for a specific time, during which you acquire the rights at a specified price for one or many uses of the copyright; for example, you might have the option to produce a feature film or a stage play. In order to enter into an option agreement, you must first decide on some essential points, such as:

- How will you exercise the option?
- What is the duration of the option?
- What is the cost to acquire the rights?
- What rights are covered by the option?
- What will be included in the screen credits, etc.?

At this point, we must talk about independent productions and union or guild productions.

What are Guilds?

A **guild** is an association of people with similar interests, or a company of equals with the same goal. It is an entity that oversees the practice of a craft or trade in a particular area. It is an association, a board, a fellowship.

The concept of guilds is known to have existed since Roman times (*collegium*, *collegia*, or *corpus*) and is the basis of what, in some cases, is called a union.

Being a member of such an association has its benefits since, as a collective, it has more bargaining power than an individual in negotiating agreements with third parties. Among other activities a guild enforces collective agreements, resolves disputes and advocates on behalf of its members, maintains an accurate directory of members, and so on.

When the budget of a production exceeds a certain amount, agreements must be negotiated with the guilds, using their collective agreements as a base. If the budget is under that figure, it is not mandatory to involve the guild.

For reference and for samples of their collective agreements, please refer directly to their websites. The following are some of the most important:

In the USA:

https://www.sagaftra.org/

https://www.dga.org/

https://www.wgaeast.org/

https://www.wga.org/

In Canada:

https://www.actra.ca/

https://www.dgc.ca/en/national/

https://www.wgc.ca/

https://cmpa.ca/

Parts of an Option Agreement

Option and purchase agreements are the foundation of any audiovisual property and must be entered into in order to avoid problems later. Below I have provided a sample of these types of agreements.

Here you will also find the writer's agreement and the story editor agreement, both of which are pivotal agreements regarding rights and their uses.

An option agreement includes the following parts:

- **Parties to the agreement.** Names and describes the legal status of the producer and creator or writer.
- **Date of the agreement.** This is important. Normally the agreement will start on the day of signing.
- **Description of the optioned work.** Describe the work that you are optioning. Is it a design, a script, a series, a movie? Give as many details as possible.
- **Rights optioned.** What is the right you are optioning? What do you want to do with those rights? Is this a series, movie, miniseries, animated show, etc.?
- **Option period (term) and renewal.** For how long you are optioning the idea or script, and what happens in the event that you are not able to procure all the necessary funds for production?
- **Credit.** Indicate how/to what extent the creator will be credited on screen and on advertising materials.
- **Initial and renewal option fee.** How much you are paying for the option to the property, and what is the amount to be paid in case of option renewal?
- **Exercise price (purchase price/acquisition price).** How much would you be paying for the execution of the option agreement, and therefore the purchase fee for the transfer of rights and purchase?
- **Writer's obligations.** What will be the creator's duties? Is she/he going to be hired as a writer or not? What would be his or her position in the production, if any?
- **Writer representations, standard warranties, and indemnities.** The writer must confirm that he or she is the sole owner of the copyright, that the property does not have any lien against it, nor there is any dispute regarding the property, nor have any of the rights to be transferred already been transferred to a third party.
- **Dispute resolution.** Describes the jurisdiction and legal system law under which the agreement has been signed and any disputes would be resolved.
- **Termination.** What happens in the case that the producer is not able to find the necessary finances to produce the show? How, when, and under which circumstances are the rights returned?
- **Certification of authorship.** Certification of the copyright of the work, registration in a guild, or similar items.

Option and Purchase Agreement Sample

[Company letterhead]

[Creator's Address]
Creator's Name
Street Address
City, State or Province
Country
Email
Phone Number

[Location and Date]
Toronto, [Month and Day], 20__

Reference: [Insert name of copyright]

Dear _____,

By this letter agreement, you confirm that you are the sole creator and exclusive author of the copyrighted work entitled "_____" (the "Work") and authorize _____ (the "Producer") for _____ years commencing as of the date of this Agreement, being the date set out above (the "Term") to use its resources and all reasonable endeavors and good business judgment to market, presell, distribute and exploit the proposed television series based on and/or inspired by the Work (the "Series") to all viable investors, producers, buyers, distributors, and, in general, any potential interested party, to secure the required funding in total on a cash flow basis for the production of the Series.

In this regard, you will grant the Producer immediate access to all materials created or existing on or before the date of this Agreement with respect to the Work and/or the Series.

The Producer will pay for all costs incurred during the Term or, if terminated prior to the end of the Term, the date of termination of this Agreement, for the purpose of developing the Series including, without limitation, costs related to research, travel, finance options, international market opportunities, further writing and creative work, creation of a one-sheet or flyer, the Producer's overhead and accounting, and legal and producing services.

It is agreed that you will have a screen credit as "Original idea by" on each episode of the series that is produced. This credit shall not be shared with any other party.

As consideration for the rights granted by you to the Producer pursuant to this Agreement, (the "Rights") you agree that the Producer shall:

1.(a) subject to Securing sufficient third-party development financing for the Series, pay to you an amount equal to $_____ as an option fee.
(b) pay to you an amount equal to ___% of the budget as Scriptwriter for each episode of the Series produced (if any), provided that such amount will be no less than $_____ per episode produced.
(c) pay to you royalties equivalent to ___% of the net revenues received by the Producer after the full production cost has been recouped.

2. As the creator of the Work you represent, warrant and covenant, and acknowledge that the Producer is entering into this Agreement in reliance on such representations, warranties and covenants, that:
(a) the Work is wholly original and was solely created by you;
(b) the exploitation of the Rights by the Producer or any other person or entity so authorized by the Producer will not infringe the copyright or any other right of any person or entity, or breach any obligation of confidentiality;
(c) no other permission or consent is required for you to grant the Rights to the Producer.

3. The parties will review this Agreement on a date to be mutually agreed upon during the Term, at which time either:
(a) The parties may mutually agree in writing to an extension of the Term; or
(b) The Producer submits to you an offer to produce the Series, and you confirm your acceptance of such an offer before the expiry of the Term.
If neither of the above two courses of action is agreed upon, this Agreement will terminate at the end of the Term.

4. Either party may terminate this Agreement by written notice to the other party if that other party:
(a) is in material breach of the terms of this Agreement and does not remedy such breach, if capable of remedy, within 14 days of being notified to do so by the terminating party; or
(b) goes into liquidation, administration, receivership, insolvency, or suffers any similar insolvency process which affords it protection from its creditors or any similar procedure in any other country in the world.

If this Agreement terminates for any reason, including, without limitation, the reasons set forth above, the Producer will acquire no equity, distribution or other rights in the Work and/or the Series and you shall retain all interest therein (including copyright, trademark, etc.) without any obligation to the Producer.

5. Prior to commencing production, you and the Producer will negotiate, in good faith, and execute a formal agreement consistent with the terms of this Agreement and industry custom and practice. The terms of such a production agreement shall be negotiated in good faith between the parties and will be subject to the mutual approval of both parties, including, without limitation, the applicable production fees, your position or back split/benefits share, and the treatment of production expenses for the Series.

6. This Letter Agreement shall not be construed as, or constitute a partnership or an association between you and the Producer, other than a contractual relationship for the purpose of the production of the Series as provided herein, and neither party shall be entitled to act on behalf of the other party and, in particular, neither party shall be entitled to enter into binding obligations on behalf of the other party.

7. In the event of any dispute, claim, question, or difference arising out of or relating to this Agreement or the breach thereof, the parties shall make their best efforts to settle such disputes, claims, questions, or differences. To this effect, we shall consult and negotiate with each other, in good faith and understanding of our respective and mutual interests, to reach a just and equitable solution satisfactory to both parties promptly upon notice by either party specifying full particulars of the dispute and, if we do not reach such solution within thirty (30) days thereafter, then either party may deliver written notice to the other party requiring resolution, by judicial process, and thereafter refer the dispute, claim, question or difference in issue to the Courts of the Province of Ontario, Canada or, if within its exclusive jurisdiction, the Federal Court of Canada, and the decision of such Courts shall be binding on both parties.

IN WITNESS WHEREOF, the parties have executed this Agreement, effective as of the date set out above.

_____
SIGNED:
For and on behalf of
Production Company.

_____
DATE:

_____
SIGNED:
Creator

_____
DATE:

Chapter 5
ASSIGNMENTS

Introduction

At this point we, as producers, hold the rights to develop a property; however, in order to develop the outline, the scripts, the story and the other creative elements, we need to hire a large number of professionals who will help us to produce the show, from directors, to cast, to musicians, editors, etc.

The hiring of this cast and crew results in new rights being created as a result of their work. As a rule of thumb, assume that anyone who is involved in any creative aspect of the show might have rights arising from their original work. i.e., positions such as directors, actors, musicians, outline creators or writers, as we have seen previously.

Think, on the other hand, how unfair it would be for the producer, who is the one assuming the risk, investing the money, putting all the aspects of the production in place, hiring people, etc. if someone else, who has already been paid for his/her services, were also to obtain other kinds of benefits.

To avoid lawsuits and doubts about the ownership of the property and copyright, the professionals who are hired must sign a document called an assignment and waiver of rights.

This is very common, especially in North America, where common law favours the freedom of assignment, but is not possible in Europe, where the law only permits the transfer of certain rights and the creators, such as directors, the creator of the outline, scriptwriters and musicians keep their authors' rights. In fact, the transfer of moral rights is not allowed in Europe.

But what is an assignment? It is defined as the process where the assignee receives rights or benefits from the assignor. In this case, the assignor would be the professional we hire and the assignee, the producer.

There are certain conditions for an assignment:
- It must occur in the present.
- The assignor clearly has to make a statement of intent to assign certain rights to the assignee.
- Assignments are irrevocable.
- If the assignor's obligation has already been performed, then the assignment cannot be revoked.

- The assignment cannot be revoked if the assignor has received consideration; for example, payment.
- Ownership of intellectual property (but there are some special conditions attaching to the assignment of trademarks and patents).

While under the employment of a company, the rights of the employees to intellectual property created by the employees during the course of their employment are automatically assigned to the company unless otherwise agreed by the employer and employee in writing. The Employment Agreement typically confirms the assignment of all the employee's intellectual property rights, but the assignment may sometimes be done through a specific agreement called a Proprietary Information and Inventions Agreement (PIIA).

Assignment Agreement Provisions

Whether the assignment of the assignor's copyright and other rights to their original work is included in the contract for the assignor's work, an employment agreement, a Proprietary Information and Inventions Agreement, or a separate Assignment and Waiver of Rights Agreement, it must include the following provisions:

- Identification of the assignor (the party making the assignment) and the assignee (the party is receiving the assignment of the rights) by their correct and complete legal names.
- The effective date of the assignment.
- A statement that the assignor is receiving consideration (money and/or other benefits) for making the assignment.
- A clear and unambiguous statement of what rights are being assigned, and provisions confirming whether the assignment applies worldwide or is subject to any territorial restrictions, as well as whether any exceptions and/or any special conditions apply.
- A statement that the assignor is assigning all rights in the work arising from the assignor's performance of the services, including any and all intellectual property rights and moral rights, in perpetuity. That such rights are waived and are not vested in the assignor, that the assignor shall not transfer any of such rights to any other person and that the assignee is free to use the work in any way the assignee sees fit.
- An agreement by the assignor to keep all information about the show confidential and to not disclose any information provided to him/her by the assignee or anyone else involved in the production to enable the assignor to perform the assignor's services.
- Representations and warranties by the assignor that the work produced by the assignor will be original work, and nobody else has any rights to it.

- An agreement by the assignor to indemnify the assignee if the representations and warranties are not true or he/she breaches the agreement.
- A waiver and release of all rights by the assignor, including the right to bring legal action against the assignee.
- An agreement that the assignor and assignee are independent contractors and are not engaged in a joint venture or an employment relationship with each other.
- An agreement by the assignor to take any further steps necessary to ensure that the ownership of the assigned rights resides with the assignee.
- Other provisions deal with such things as the governing law jurisdiction, the fact that the agreement contains all the terms of the parties' agreement, and that amendments do not apply unless they are in writing and signed by both parties, etc.

The following is a sample of a stand-alone Assignment and Waiver of Rights Agreement allowing for an assignment and waiver of rights by the assignor (an artist) to the assignee (the producer). As with all sample agreements, it will need to be used with caution and carefully modified to suit the specific circumstances of the production.

Assignment and Waiver of Rights: Sample Agreement

ASSIGNMENT and WAIVER OF RIGHTS

WHEREAS _____(the Producer's company name) (the "Producer"), a Canadian company, incorporated in the province of _____, having its principal office at _____, Canada, is the creator and producer of an original animated show called "_____", as further described in Schedule "A" to this Assignment Agreement (the "Work"), in which the Producer owns all the copyright, including copyright in the characters and show concept;

AND WHEREAS the Producer has hired _____(the "Artist"), a citizen of_____, whose principal address is_____ as an independent contractor, to provide the following services in connection with the Work: _____(the "Services") according to the Producer's instructions;

AND WHEREAS the Producer provided the Artist with all required artwork, descriptions, information and other details for the Characters, and related backgrounds and props, including rough drawings, illustrations, thumbnail sketches, storyboards, layouts, colours, model sheets and character profiles, in which the Producer owns all the copyright and any other rights, and from which the Artist was instructed to adapt the Work.

AND WHEREAS the Artist and the Producer agree that the performance of the Services by the Artist does not and will not vest in or transfer to the Artist any rights, including copyright, in the Work, the Characters or any derivative works of the Work or the Characters, including those derivative works generated by the Artist during the course of his performance of the Services (the "Derivative Works");

AND WHEREAS the Artist agrees that all rights and interests which may accrue to him/her as a result of performing the Services belong to the Producer and this Assignment and Waiver confirms the assignment and waiver of rights as well as the future understanding between the parties;

NOW THEREFORE in consideration of the premises, the payment by the Producer to the Artist of the sum agreed upon for the performance of the Services, their respective agreements set out below and other good and valuable consideration given by each party to the other, the receipt and sufficiency of which is hereby acknowledged by each of the parties, the parties hereby agree with each other as follows:

1. ASSIGNMENT

1.1   The Artist hereby sells, assigns, transfers and conveys to the Producer in perpetuity, all rights, title and interest in and to the Work and any Derivative Works and all rights created by the Artist through the performance of the Services, and confirms he/she has sold, assigned and transferred and hereby sells, assigns and transfers to the Producer, its successors and assigns, in perpetuity, throughout the world, any and all rights, including copyright in the Work, the Characters and Derivative Works, that may accrue to the Artist, now or in future, as a result of his/her ownership and/or the performance of the Services.

1.2   The Artist further agrees without further consideration to, in future, do such further acts and execute and deliver to the Producer such further assignments, waivers, applications, documents or assurances as the Producer, acting reasonably, may request, to vest, effect, perfect, register, record, verify, evidence or enforce its rights and interests, including copyright, in the above-mentioned Work, Characters or Derivative Works.

1.3   It is hereby further acknowledged by the Artist that the Producer, as sole owner of all rights in the Work, the Characters and the Derivative Works, may, without further agreement of, or compensation to, the Artist, use or alter the Derivative Works generated by the Artist as they sees fit in their absolute discretion, including but not limited to the reproduction, public performance, public telecommunication or dissemination of the Work by electronic means and/or by any other means or medium, now known or hereafter devised, including the combination of the Work, Characters, or Derivative Works with any other literary, artistic, dramatic or musical work for use in a multimedia product or otherwise.

1.4   The Artist further waives and agrees in future to waive, in favour of the Producer, any and all moral rights, if any, of its successors, assigns, agents, representatives, officers, employees, and any other third parties acting under its authority, for their full term, throughout the world, that may accrue to him from performing the Services in respect to the Work, the Characters and/or the Derivative Works, including his right to be associated with the Work, the Characters or the Derivative Works, and to be named in the credits for an episode of the Work, created now or in the future.

1.5   The parties hereto agree that the copyright in respect to the Work, the Characters, the Derivative Works, or any underlying materials, may be registered throughout the world by the Producer at the discretion of the Producer, in the name of the Producer.

2. CONFIDENTIAL INFORMATION

2.1   The Artist agrees that all materials or information, whether given orally or in writing, about the Work or the Characters, and related backgrounds and props, including rough drawings, illustrations, thumbnail sketches, storyboards, layouts, colours, model sheets, and character profiles, which are disclosed to the Artist by the Producer during the course of the Artist's performance of the Services, shall be treated as confidential information owned by the Producer, and the Artist shall not, during or after the period of his performance of the Services, disclose to any person or use for his own benefit or the benefit of anyone, nor allow the disclosure or use by anyone else, of such confidential information without the prior written consent of the Producer.

2.2   The Artist further agrees that all materials or information, whether given orally or in writing, about new works other than the Work, including other series, characters, and related backgrounds and props, including rough drawings, illustrations, thumbnail sketches, storyboards, layouts, colours, model sheets, and character profiles, which are disclosed to the Artist by the Producer or any agent, director, officer, employee, contractor or other representative of the Producer during the course of the Artist's performance of the Services, shall be treated as confidential information owned by the Producer and the Artist shall not, during or after the period of his performance of the Services, disclose to any person or use for his own benefit or the benefit of anyone else, or allow the disclosure or use by anyone else, of such confidential information without the prior written consent of the Producer.

2.3   Upon request by the Producer or on completion of the Services by the Artist, the Artist further agrees to deliver the Work promptly to the Producer and to erase all electronic copies of any and all documents or other materials in his possession or under his control, whose subject matter relates to the Work, the Characters, related backgrounds, and props, or the Derivative Works, including but not limited to rough drawings, clean-up drawings, illustrations, thumbnail sketches, storyboards, layouts, colours, model sheets, character profiles, and any copies in any form of media made thereof which the Artist may have made, may have access to or may receive or have received, possessed or maintained control over, during the period of his discussions or business relationship with the Producer. If required by the Producer, the Artist agrees to provide a sworn statement that no copies of such documents or materials have been retained by the Artist.

3. REPRESENTATIONS AND WARRANTIES

3.1   The Artist represents, warrants, and covenants to the Producer that he is the sole technical adaptor of the Characters and all artistic material, and that his technical adaptations are original, except to the extent that his adaptations are based upon the Characters, and related backgrounds and props, including rough drawings, illustrations, thumbnail sketches, storyboards, layouts, colours, model sheets and/or character profiles provided by the Producer, and that the technical adaptations of the Characters or any other content of the Derivative Works generated by the Artist do not and will not infringe upon any proprietary rights or interests of any other person, nor are or will they be obscene or otherwise unlawful, nor has the Artist licensed, transferred or in any other way encumbered any rights in and to his works of the Characters or any other content of the Derivative Works that would conflict with this Assignment Agreement.

4. INDEMNITY

4.1   The Artist shall indemnify the Producer in respect to any losses, damages, expenses, and costs, including reasonable legal fees and disbursements, arising from any claim, complaint, or action arising from any breach or alleged breach of any of the Artist's agreements, warranties and/or representations contained herein.

4.2   The Artist shall have no right to terminate this Agreement. The Artist shall have no right to enjoin the exploitation of any media by the Producer of the rights in the Work, Characters, or Derivative Works assigned to the Producer hereunder or to obtain injunctive relief of any kind in connection therewith.

5. WAIVER AND RELEASE

5.1   The Artist agrees that he will not commence any legal action against the Producer, its officers, directors, shareholders, servants, employees, successors, assigns, licensees or partners, in any jurisdiction in the world, in respect to any rights or interests, including copyright, which may have accrued to him in regards to the Work, the Characters or the Derivative Works as a result of his performance of the Services, or against any future uses of the Work, Characters or the Derivative Works by the Producer or any of its successors, assigns, licensees or partners, including but not limited to any reproduction, public performance, public telecommunication or dissemination of the Work, the Characters or the Derivative Works by electronic means and by any other means or medium, now known or hereafter devised, and hereby irrevocably waives any right to take such legal actions.

5.2   The Artist hereby and forever releases the Producer, its officers, directors, shareholders, servants, employees, successors, assigns, licensees or partners, from all past, present or future claims, demands, suits, actions, matters or causes of action, executions, bonds, indemnities, or other obligations of any kind or nature, which he may have had, or will have, arising out of, or in any way connected to, his agreement with the Producer to perform the Services.

6. SUCCESSORS, LICENSEES & ASSIGNS

6.1   The Producer shall be entitled to assign, license, or otherwise dispose of or deal in whole or in part with the benefit of this Assignment Agreement and any of its additional rights hereunder to any person, firm or company, and the assignment and the covenants, agreements, and warranties by the Artist herein contained shall apply to the benefit of any such assignee, licensee or successor of the Producer.

7. RELATIONSHIP BETWEEN THE PARTIES

7.1   The Artist acknowledges that he does not have the authority, and is not entitled, to commit or bind the Producer to any matter, contract, or negotiation.

7.2   The parties will be free to perform consulting, co-productions and other Services to or for other clients and/or partners during the term of this Agreement; provided, however, that the Artist shall ensure that he is able to perform the Services in a timely manner in accordance with the terms of this Agreement.

7.3   The parties agree that the Artist has been hired by the Producer as an independent contractor and that nothing in this Assignment Agreement shall be deemed to constitute a partnership or joint venture between the parties, and neither of them shall do or allow to be done, anything whereby it shall or may be represented that one of the parties is a partner of, or in a joint venture with, the other party. The Artist and the Producer further acknowledge that the Artist is not an employee of the Producer and that the Producer shall not withhold and remit income taxes, Canada Pension Plan and Employment Insurance assessments and/or other payroll deductions and/or any similar deductions or payments in respect to the compensation payable by the Producer to the Artist for the performance of the Services. The Artist acknowledges that he is solely responsible for all such payments and/or remittances.

7.4   If any provision of this Agreement is determined to be invalid or unenforceable in whole or in part under any applicable statute or the rule of law by a court of competent jurisdiction, such provision shall be, to that extent, deemed omitted and such invalidity or unenforceability shall attach only to such provision, or part of such provision and the remaining part of such provision and all other provisions of it shall continue in full force and effect.

7.5   The Producer and the Artist each individually warrant that they are free to enter into and fully perform this Agreement.

7.6   Each of the parties to this Agreement agrees to execute any additional documents which may be required to fully effectuate the purposes and intents of this Agreement or to carry out the obligations of the parties hereunder provided that they are consistent with the provisions of this Agreement.

7.7   The parties hereby acknowledge receipt of a copy of this Agreement, duly signed by the other parties. Each of the parties confirms that such party has read this Agreement, understood it, had the opportunity to obtain independent legal advice about it prior to executing this Agreement, and agrees to its terms.

7.8   The parties hereby agree that they shall not incur any obligations in respect to any other party, and nothing in this agreement is intended or should be construed so as to give any right or benefit to any third party as against either or both of the parties.

7.9   Each party to this Agreement hereby acknowledges that no representation or warranty not expressly set forth in this Agreement has been made to the other party.

7.10   This agreement constitutes the entire understanding of the parties at the date hereof with respect to the subject matter hereof and supersedes all prior agreements arrangements and understandings between the parties relating thereto, whether oral or in writing. Any amendments or variations thereto must be in writing and signed by duly authorized representatives of the parties hereto.

7.11 No waiver express or implied by one party hereto of a breach by the other party of any of the provisions of this Agreement shall operate as a waiver of any preceding or succeeding breach of the same or any other provision of this Agreement.

8. INTERPRETATION

8.1 Terms and conditions set out in this Agreement or in any Schedule hereto, which are usual in the industry in Canada, shall be interpreted in accordance with customary industry practices unless the context otherwise requires or the parties otherwise explicitly agree in writing.

8.2 The division of this Agreement into Articles and Sections and the insertion of headings are for convenience of reference only and shall not affect the construction or interpretation of this Agreement.

8.3 Unless the context requires otherwise, words importing the singular include the plural and vice versa and words importing gender include all genders.

8.4 Unless the context requires otherwise, references in this Agreement to Sections or Schedules are to Sections or Schedules of this Agreement.

9. GOVERNING LAW

9.1 The parties agree that the laws of the Province of Ontario, Canada, and the federal laws of Canada applicable therein, shall govern this Agreement, and the relationship and rights, including copyright, of the parties hereunder, and the courts of the Province of Ontario and, on matters within its jurisdiction, the Federal Court of Canada, shall have exclusive jurisdiction over the resolution of disputes hereunder or relating thereto and all legal proceedings to enforce the rights of a party under this Agreement and each of the parties attorns to the jurisdiction of such courts.

EXECUTED at _____, this _____ day of _____, 20XX.

[Schedule A will start on a new page of the document.]

<u>SCHEDULE "A" to the ASSIGNMENT and WAIVER OF RIGHTS</u>
by the Artist to the Producer

For the purposes of this ASSIGNMENT and WAIVER OF RIGHTS "Work" shall be defined to include, but not limited to any and all: Characters, BG, props, logos, identities, fonts, rough drawings, illustrations, thumbnail sketches, storyboards, layouts, colours, model sheets, and character profiles and SFX in any form of any animated series, animated shorts, animated feature films, in any system, CGI, traditional animation, computer-assisted animation, etc. developed and/or produced by the Producer entitled "_____" (which, together with the title, themes, contents and characters and all drafts, transcripts, outlines, notes, translations, adaptations and other versions thereof, whether now existing or hereafter created, is hereinafter called the "Property"), during the term of this Assignment Agreement with the Artist and also shall apply after expiration or termination of the Assignment Agreement in perpetuity.

Chapter 6
NON-DISCLOSURE AND NON-CIRCUMVENTION AGREEMENTS

Introduction

This chapter discusses some other necessary steps you may need to take to protect your idea. You do not want anyone to talk about your project without having all the relevant information, nor do you want anyone to share key information that will allow someone else to copy or modify your concept.

To avoid these situations, there are certain types of agreements that will protect you. One type of agreement is a **non-disclosure agreement (NDA)**, also called a **proprietary information agreement (PIA)**, **confidential disclosure agreement (CDA)**, **confidentiality agreement (CA)**, or **secrecy agreement (SA)**.

Types of Non-Disclosure Agreements

Non-disclosure agreements may apply to a single party (unilateral) or be mutual, including two (bilateral) or several parties (multi-party).

Which type of agreement is needed will depend on the circumstances.

- If one party is disclosing confidential information to another party, the party receiving the information will need to sign a unilateral (one-way) NDA, agreeing to keep the disclosed information confidential.

- If two parties are disclosing confidential information to each other or sharing information, a mutual, bilateral (two-way) NDA (MNDA) is needed. In that agreement, each party will agree to keep the other party's information confidential and to not disclose it, except for the purpose of carrying out their joint project.

- If several parties are involved in a project, and they will be sharing confidential information with the other parties, a mutual, multilateral NDA (MNDA), which involves three or more parties, is needed. Each party will agree with each of the other parties to keep the information received from the others confidential.

Purposes of Non-Disclosure Agreements

Basically, a non-disclosure agreement is signed by the person who will see your property for the first time. In it, the person receiving the property must agree not to disclose any information about the confidential and/or proprietary materials that have been provided to them and to only use the confidential information for the purpose of carrying out the project, as specified in the agreement. Nothing, *absolutely nothing*, can be said or shared regarding what you have seen without the explicit permission of the disclosing party.

You will see in the samples provided below how vital this agreement can be. It is used, for example, when a client shows something to the production crew that will be working on the project. If a crew member leaks the idea or concept to someone else who exploits it, your project may be irreparably damaged.

Non-Circumvention Agreements

There is another type of agreement that not everyone requests, the **non-circumvention agreement**. This protects certain transactions between the parties that may require and result in the introduction of third parties. The non-circumvention agreement includes prohibitions on a party taking actions or working out arrangements with a third party that result in another party being deprived of commissions, royalties, or other payments to which that party should be entitled.

Sample Agreements

The following sample agreements are provided as general guidance and must be modified according to the circumstances. In particular, the definition of "confidential information" in an agreement should specify the information or type of information that will or may be disclosed and the particular purposes for which one or more other parties are receiving the confidential information. Depending on what other agreements are being entered into by the parties, it may be necessary to include other provisions. It is essential to ensure that the agreement clearly sets out what the parties have agreed to and accurately reflects the arrangements between the parties. Obtaining proper legal advice from an experienced lawyer is always recommended.

Three sample NDAs (unilateral, bilateral and multi-lateral) have been provided, along with a sample of a non-circumvention agreement.

NONDISCLOSURE AGREEMENT – SINGLE PARTY (UNILATERAL)

This NonDisclosure Agreement ("Agreement") is entered into as of [DATE] between:
[NAME OF PRODUCER] ("Producer"), a corporation incorporated under the laws of [INCORPORATING JURISDICTION], having its principal office at [ADDRESS];
and
[NAME OF OTHER PARTY] ("Covenantor"), a corporation incorporated under the laws of [INCORPORATING JURISDICTION], having its principal office at [ADDRESS].

Recitals

A) The Producer is entering into discussions with the Covenantor concerning the following production project: [SHORT DESCRIPTION OF PROJECT] (the "Project") for the purpose of determining whether the Producer will engage the Covenantor to provide the following services: [SHORT DESCRIPTION OF SERVICES] (the "Services") in connection with the Project;

B) It will be necessary for the Producer to disclose Confidential Information (as defined below) to the Covenantor during such discussions and, if the Producer and the Covenantor agree to enter into a service contract for the Project (the "Service Contract"), further disclosures of Confidential Information will be required;

C) It is essential to the Producer that all Confidential Information disclosed by it to the Covenantor be kept strictly and absolutely confidential, and it has therefore required that the Covenantor enters into this agreement (the "Agreement") with respect to the Confidential Information.

Consideration

In consideration of the disclosures to be made by the Producer, and other good and valuable consideration, the receipt and sufficiency of which is expressly acknowledged by the Covenantor, the Covenantor covenants and agrees with the Producer as follows:

Definition of Confidential Information

1. As used in this Agreement, "Confidential Information" means any and all information and material concerning the Producer and/or the Project (whether prepared by the Producer, or otherwise) that is furnished to the Covenantor (orally, in writing, or electronically) by or on behalf of the Producer and any material, information or work developed, derived or resulting therefrom, including, without limitation, summaries, notes, books, stories, scripts, proposals for film or television productions, names and/or descriptions of characters, marketing, and project development plans, technical

information, business, and financial data, intellectual property of any nature, website designs, internet marketing or sales practices or strategies, and records of any type containing or otherwise reflecting such information or material.

The Producer acknowledges that "Confidential Information" does not include:

(a) information or material already known to the Covenantor or in its possession, with no obligation to keep it confidential, at the time of its receipt from the Producer;
(b) information or material received by the Covenantor in good faith from a third party lawfully in possession of it and have no obligation to keep it confidential;
(c) information publicly known at the time of its receipt by the Covenantor or which has become publicly known through methods other than by a breach of this Agreement or other action by the Covenantor or any of its directors, officers, employees, contractors or other representatives (the "Covenantor's Representatives"); or
(d) information or material independently developed by the Covenantor without reference to the Confidential Information for purposes other than the Project and/or the provision of the Services and without violating this Agreement.

Confidentiality and Non-Disclosure Obligations of the Covenantor

2. The Covenantor shall hold in confidence and use the Confidential Information solely for the purpose of participating in discussions with the Producer concerning the Project, including developing proposals for the Services to be provided by the Covenantor, and carrying out its obligations to the Producer under the Service Contract if entered into, and for no other purpose whatsoever. The Covenantor shall not, during the continuance of this Agreement or at any time thereafter, without the prior written authorization of the Producer, (i) disclose any of the Confidential Information to any person other than Covenantor's Representatives who require such information for the purposes of participating in the discussions relating to the Project or providing the Services, or (ii) copy, reproduce or release, directly or in any form, any Confidential Information or any work derived or resulting therefrom.

3. The Covenantor acknowledges that the Producer is not under any obligation to enter into a Service Contract with it and that either of them may terminate their discussions at any time and for any reason prior to the entering into of a Service Contract. The Covenantor agrees to return promptly to the Producer or destroy (subject only to the Covenantor's legal obligations to retain records required for tax or other financial purposes) any copies, including all derivations, of Confidential Information in written or another tangible form upon request of the Producer or once the use of such information, to the limited extent permitted by this Agreement, is complete or upon termination of the parties' discussions without the execution of a Service Contract.

4. The Covenantor shall cause each of the Covenantor's affiliated, subsidiary and associated corporations and the Covenantor's Representatives to comply with the Covenantor's obligations under this Agreement and shall be fully responsible and liable to the Producer for any and all breaches of or failures to comply with this Agreement by such corporations and/or the Covenantor's Representatives, whether or not the Covenantor had knowledge of such breach or non-compliance.

5. The Covenantor acknowledges that its obligations under this Agreement with regard to the Confidential Information shall continue to be in effect after the execution of a Service Contract.

6. If the Covenantor commits a default or breach of its obligations under this Agreement, the Producer shall be entitled to terminate this Agreement immediately and recover all costs (including legal expenses) incurred in enforcing or protecting its rights under this Agreement.

7. The Covenantor acknowledges that any breach of the covenants contained in this Agreement may cause the Producer irreparable harm, and remedies at law for any such breach may be inadequate. Accordingly, the Producer shall be entitled to seek to obtain a restraining order, injunction, or another similar remedy (without any requirement to post a bond as a condition of such relief) for any breach or threatened breach of this Agreement by the Covenantor. Nothing contained in this Agreement shall be construed as limiting either party's right to any other remedies at law, including the recovery of damages for breach of this Agreement.

General Provisions

8. Neither party may assign this Agreement without the prior written consent of the other party. Subject to that restriction, this Agreement shall be binding upon and inure to the benefit of the parties and their respective successors and assigns. A waiver by either of the parties of any breach by the other party of any of the terms, provisions or conditions of this Agreement or the acquiescence of either party in any act (whether of commission or omission) which but for such acquiescence would be a breach as aforesaid, shall not constitute a general waiver of such term, provision, or condition for any subsequent act contrary thereto.

9. This Agreement and the Service Contract (if and when executed) represent the entire understanding between the parties with respect to the subject matter of this Agreement and supersede all prior written or oral agreements made by or on behalf of the Covenantor or the Producer with respect to such subject matter. Any amendment or modification to this Agreement must be in writing and signed by both parties.

10. If any provision of this Agreement is declared invalid by a court of competent jurisdiction, such provision shall be ineffective only to the extent of such invalidity, so that the remainder of that provision and all remaining provisions of this Agreement will continue in full force and effect.

11. This Agreement, the relationship of the parties, and any disputes relating to this Agreement shall be governed by and construed and interpreted in accordance with the laws of the Province of Ontario and the federal laws of Canada applicable in that province. Any action or proceeding to this Agreement shall be instituted in an Ontario court, or, if within its exclusive jurisdiction, the Federal Court of Canada and the decisions of such court(s) shall be binding on both parties.

12. The Covenantor acknowledges receipt of a copy of this Agreement, duly signed by the Covenantor. The Covenantor, through its directors and officers, has read this Agreement, understands it, has had the opportunity to obtain independent legal advice about it prior to executing this Agreement, and agrees to its terms. If signed by an electronic signature, the Covenantor agrees to be bound by its own electronic signature, and the Producer agrees that it accepts the electronic signature of the Covenantor.

IN WITNESS WHEREOF, the Covenantor has caused this Agreement to be executed by its duly authorized representative.

[NAME OF COVENANTOR]

By: _____
    Name:
    Title:

I have the authority to bind the Corporation.

[End of this sample agreement.]

NONDISCLOSURE AGREEMENT – TWO PARTY (MUTUAL, BILATERAL)

This NonDisclosure Agreement ("Agreement") is entered into as of [DATE] between:
[NAME OF PRODUCER] ("Producer"), a corporation incorporated under the laws of [INCORPORATING JURISDICTION], having its principal office at [ADDRESS];
and
[NAME OF OTHER PARTY] ("Company"), a corporation incorporated under the laws of [INCORPORATING JURISDICTION], having its principal office at [ADDRESS].

Recitals

A)   The Producer and the Company are entering into discussions concerning the following production project: [SHORT DESCRIPTION OF PROJECT] (the "Project") for the purpose of determining whether the Producer and the Company will enter into an agreement (a "Service Contract") for the provision by the Company of the following services: [SHORT DESCRIPTION OF SERVICES] (the "Services") in connection with the Project;

B)   It will be necessary for each of the Producer and the Company to disclose Confidential Information (as defined below) to each other during such discussions and, if a Service Contract is entered into for the Project, further disclosures of Confidential Information will be required;

C)   It is essential to each of the Producer and the Company that all Confidential Information disclosed by either of them to the other party be kept strictly and absolutely confidential, and the parties have therefore agreed to enter into this agreement (the "Agreement") with respect to the Confidential Information.

Consideration

In consideration of the disclosures to be made by each party to the other party, their mutual agreements set out in this Agreement and other good and valuable consideration, the receipt and sufficiency of which is expressly acknowledged by each of the parties, the Producer and the Company covenant and agree with each other as follows:

Definition of Confidential Information

1. As used in this Agreement, "Confidential Information" means any and all information and material concerning or relating to the party disclosing such information and material (the "Disclosing Party") and/or the Project (whether prepared by the Disclosing Party, or otherwise) that is furnished to the other party (the "Receiving Party"), orally, in writing, or electronically or in any other manner by or on behalf of the Disclosing

Party and any material, information or work developed, derived or resulting therefrom, including, without limitation, summaries, notes, books, stories, scripts, proposals for film or television productions, names and/or descriptions of characters, marketing, and project development plans, technical information, business, and financial data, intellectual property of any nature, website designs, internet marketing or sales practices or strategies, and records of any type containing or otherwise reflecting such information or material.

Each of the parties acknowledges that "Confidential Information" does not include:

(a) information or material already known to the Receiving Party or in its possession, without obligation to keep it confidential, at the time of its receipt from the Disclosing Party;
(b) information or material received by the Receiving Party in good faith from a third party lawfully in possession of it and have no obligation to keep it confidential;
(c) information publicly known at the time of its receipt by the Receiving Party or which has become publicly known through methods other than by a breach of this Agreement or other action by the Receiving Party or any of its directors, officers, employees, contractors or other representatives (the "Receiving Party's Representatives"); or
(d) information or material independently developed by the Receiving Party without reference to the Confidential Information for purposes other than the Project and/or the provision of the Services and without violating this Agreement.

Confidentiality and Non-Disclosure Obligations

2. The Receiving Party shall hold in confidence and use the Confidential Information solely for the purpose of participating in discussions with the Disclosing Party concerning the Project, including developing proposals for the Services to be provided by the Receiving Party, and carrying out its obligations to the Disclosing Party if a Service Contract is entered into, and for no other purpose whatsoever. The Receiving Party shall not, during the continuance of this Agreement or at any time thereafter, without the prior written authorization of the Disclosing Party, (i) disclose any of the Confidential Information to any person other than Receiving Party's Representatives who require such information for the purposes of participating in the discussions relating to the Project or providing the Services, or (ii) copy, reproduce or release, directly or in any form, any Confidential Information or any work derived or resulting therefrom.

3. The parties acknowledge that they are not under any obligation to enter into a Service Contract and that either of them may terminate their discussions at any time and for any reason prior to the entering into of a Service Contract. The Receiving Party agrees to return promptly to the Disclosing Party or destroy (subject only to the

Receiving Party's legal obligations to retain records required for tax or other financial purposes) any copies, including all derivations, of Confidential Information in written or other tangible form upon request of the Disclosing Party or once the use of such information, to the limited extent permitted by this Agreement, is complete or upon termination of the parties' discussions without the execution of a Service Contract.

4. The Receiving Party shall cause each of its affiliated, subsidiary and associated corporations and the Receiving Party's Representatives to comply with the Receiving Party's obligations under this Agreement and shall be fully responsible and liable to the Disclosing Party for any and all breaches of or failures to comply with this Agreement by one or more of such corporations and/or the Receiving Party's Representatives, whether or not the Receiving Party had knowledge of such breach or non-compliance.

5. Each of the parties acknowledges that its obligations under this Agreement with regard to the Confidential Information shall continue to be in effect after the execution of a Service Contract.

6. If either party commits a default or breach of its material obligations under this Agreement, the other party shall be entitled to terminate this Agreement immediately and recover all reasonable costs (including legal expenses) incurred in enforcing or protecting its rights under this Agreement.

7. The Receiving Party acknowledges that any breach of the covenants contained in this Agreement may cause the Disclosing Party irreparable harm, and remedies at law for any such breach may be inadequate. Accordingly, the Disclosing Party shall be entitled to seek to obtain a restraining order, injunction, or another similar remedy (without any requirement to post a bond as a condition of such relief) for any breach or threatened breach of this Agreement by the Receiving Party. Nothing contained in this Agreement shall be construed as limiting either party's right to any other remedies at law, including the recovery of damages for breach of this Agreement.

General Provisions

8. Neither party may assign this Agreement without the prior written consent of the other party. Subject to that restriction, this Agreement shall be binding upon and inure to the benefit of the parties and their respective successors and permitted assigns. A waiver by either of the parties of any breach by the other party of any of the terms, provisions or conditions of this Agreement or the acquiescence of either party in any act (whether of commission or omission) which but for such acquiescence would be a breach as aforesaid, shall not constitute a general waiver of such term, provision or condition for any subsequent act contrary thereto.

9. This Agreement and the Service Contract (if and when executed) represent the entire understanding between the parties with respect to the subject matter of this Agreement and supersede all prior written or oral agreements made by or on behalf of the parties with respect to such subject matter. Any amendment or modification to this Agreement must be in writing and signed by both parties.

10. If any provision of this Agreement is declared invalid by a court of competent jurisdiction, such provision shall be ineffective only to the extent of such invalidity, so that the remainder of that provision and all remaining provisions of this Agreement will continue in full force and effect.

11. This Agreement, the relationship of the parties, and any disputes relating to this Agreement shall be governed by and construed and interpreted in accordance with the laws of the Province of Ontario and the federal laws of Canada applicable in that province. Any action or proceeding to this Agreement shall be instituted in an Ontario court, or, if within its exclusive jurisdiction, the Federal Court of Canada and the decisions of such court(s) shall be binding on both parties.

12. Each of the parties acknowledges receipt of a copy of this Agreement, duly signed by the other party and acknowledges that, through its directors and officers, it has read this Agreement, understands it, has had the opportunity to obtain independent legal advice about it prior to executing this Agreement, and agrees to its terms. If signed by an electronic signature, each of the parties agrees to be bound by its own electronic signature and to accept the electronic signature of the other party.

IN WITNESS WHEREOF, each of the parties has caused this Agreement to be executed by its duly authorized representative.

[NAME OF PRODUCER]

By: _____
    Name:
    Title:

I have authority to bind the Corporation.

[NAME OF COMPANY]

By: _____
    Name:
    Title:

I have authority to bind the Corporation.

[End of this sample agreement.]

NONDISCLOSURE AGREEMENT – MULTIPLE PARTIES
(MUTUAL, MULTILATERAL)

This NonDisclosure Agreement ("Agreement") is entered into as of [DATE] between:
[NAME OF PRODUCER] ("Producer"), a corporation incorporated under the laws of [INCORPORATING JURISDICTION], having its principal office at [ADDRESS];
and
[NAME OF OTHER PARTY 1] ("Company 1"), a corporation incorporated under the laws of [INCORPORATING JURISDICTION], having its principal office at [ADDRESS];
and
[NAME OF OTHER PARTY 2] ("Company 2"), a corporation incorporated under the laws of [INCORPORATING JURISDICTION], having its principal office at [ADDRESS].
[Any number of additional parties may be added]

Recitals

A)   The Producer, Company 1 and Company 2 [AND OTHER PARTIES IF APPLICABLE] (the parties other than the Producer being referred to collectively as the "Companies") are entering into discussions concerning the following production project: [SHORT DESCRIPTION OF PROJECT] (the "Project") for the purpose of determining whether the Producer and one or more of the Companies will enter into one or more agreements (a "Service Contract") for the provision by one or more of the Companies of services (the "Services") in connection with the Project;

B)   It will be necessary for each of the parties to disclose Confidential Information (as defined below) to one or more of the other parties during such discussions and, if a Service Contract is entered into for the Project by two or more of the parties, further disclosures of Confidential Information will be required;

C)   It is essential to each of the parties that all Confidential Information disclosed by any of them to one or more of the other parties be kept strictly and absolutely confidential, and the parties have therefore agreed to enter into this agreement (the "Agreement") with respect to the Confidential Information.

Consideration

In consideration of the disclosures to be made by each party to one or more of the other parties, their mutual agreements set out in this Agreement and other good and valuable consideration, the receipt and sufficiency of which is expressly acknowledged by each of the parties, each of the parties covenants and agrees with all of the other parties as follows:

Definition of Confidential Information

1.   As used in this Agreement, "Confidential Information" means any and all information and material concerning or relating to the party disclosing such information and material (the "Disclosing Party") and/or the Project (whether prepared by the Disclosing Party, or otherwise) that is furnished to one or more of the other parties (each of the parties receiving such information being referred to as the "Receiving Party"), orally, in writing, or electronically or in any other manner by or on behalf of the Disclosing Party and any material, information or work developed, derived or resulting therefrom, including, without limitation, summaries, notes, books, stories, scripts, proposals for film or television productions, names and/or descriptions of characters, marketing, and project development plans, technical information, business, and financial data, intellectual property of any nature, website designs, internet marketing or sales practices or strategies, and records of any type containing or otherwise reflecting such information or material.

Each of the parties acknowledges that "Confidential Information" does not include:

(a) information or material already known to the Receiving Party or in its possession, without obligation to keep it confidential, at the time of its receipt from the Disclosing Party;
(b) information or material received by the Receiving Party in good faith from a third party lawfully in possession of it and have no obligation to keep it confidential;
(c) information publicly known at the time of its receipt by the Receiving Party or which has become publicly known through methods other than by a breach of this Agreement or other action by the Receiving Party or any of its directors, officers, employees, contractors or other representatives (the "Receiving Party's Representatives"); or
(d) information or material independently developed by the Receiving Party without reference to the Confidential Information for purposes other than the Project and/or the provision of the Services and without violating this Agreement.

Confidentiality and Non-Disclosure Obligations

2. The Receiving Party shall hold in confidence and use the Confidential Information solely for the purpose of participating in discussions with the other parties concerning the Project, including developing proposals for the Services to be provided by the Receiving Party, and carrying out its obligations if a Service Contract is entered into, and for no other purpose whatsoever. The Receiving Party shall not, during the continuance of this Agreement or at any time thereafter, without the prior written authorization of the Disclosing Party, (i) disclose any of the Disclosing Party's Confidential Information to any person other than the Receiving Party's Representatives or the representa-

tives of another party to this Agreement who require such information for the purposes of participating in the discussions relating to the Project or providing Services, or (ii) copy, reproduce or release, directly or in any form, any Confidential Information or any work derived or resulting therefrom.

3. The parties acknowledge that none of them are under any obligation to enter into a Service Contract with the Producer or any other party and that any of them may terminate their discussions at any time and for any reason prior to the entering into of a Service Contract. Each Receiving Party agrees to return promptly to the Disclosing Party or destroy (subject only to the Receiving Party's legal obligations to retain records required for tax or other financial purposes) any copies, including all derivations, of Confidential Information in written or other tangible form upon request of the Disclosing Party or once the use of such information, to the limited extent permitted by this Agreement, is complete or upon termination of the Receiving Party's discussions without the execution of a Service Contract.

4. Each Receiving Party shall cause each of its affiliated, subsidiary and associated corporations and the Receiving Party's Representatives to comply with the Receiving Party's obligations under this Agreement and shall be fully responsible and liable to the Disclosing Party for any and all breaches of or failures to comply with this Agreement by one or more of such corporations and/or the Receiving Party's Representatives, whether or not the Receiving Party had knowledge of such breach or non-compliance.

5. Each of the parties acknowledges that its obligations under this Agreement with regard to the Confidential Information shall continue in effect after the execution of a Service Contract.

6. If any party commits a default or breach of its obligations under this Agreement (the "Defaulting Party"), the party or parties claiming to be damaged by such breach shall be entitled to terminate all discussions with the Defaulting Party immediately by written notice to the Defaulting Party and to initiate proceedings to recover all reasonable costs (including legal expenses) incurred in enforcing or protecting its rights under this Agreement. Any such action shall not terminate this Agreement.

7. Each Receiving Party acknowledges that any breach of the covenants contained in this Agreement may cause the Disclosing Party irreparable harm, and remedies at law for any such breach may be inadequate. Accordingly, the Disclosing Party shall be entitled to seek to obtain a restraining order, injunction, or another similar remedy (without any requirement to post a bond as a condition of such relief) for any breach or threatened breach of this Agreement by one or more Receiving Parties. Nothing contained in this Agreement shall be construed as limiting any party's right to any other remedies at law, including the recovery of damages for breach of this Agreement.

General Provisions

8. None of the parties may assign this Agreement without the prior written consent of each of the other parties. Subject to that restriction, this Agreement shall be binding upon and inure to the benefit of the parties and their respective successors and permitted assigns. A waiver by any party of any breach by any other party of any of the terms, provisions or conditions of this Agreement or the acquiescence of a party in any act (whether of commission or omission) which but for such acquiescence would be a breach as aforesaid, shall not constitute a general waiver of such term, provision or condition for any subsequent act contrary thereto.

9. This Agreement and the Service Contracts (if and when executed) represent the entire understanding between the parties with respect to the subject matter of this Agreement and supersede all prior written or oral agreements made by or on behalf of the parties with respect to such subject matter. Any amendment or modification to this Agreement must be in writing and signed by all of the parties.

10. If any provision of this Agreement is declared invalid by a court of competent jurisdiction, such provision shall be ineffective only to the extent of such invalidity, so that the remainder of that provision and all remaining provisions of this Agreement will continue in full force and effect.

11. This Agreement, the relationship of the parties, and any disputes relating to this Agreement shall be governed by and construed and interpreted in accordance with the laws of the Province of Ontario and the federal laws of Canada applicable in that province. Any action or proceeding to this Agreement shall be instituted in an Ontario court, or, if within its exclusive jurisdiction, the Federal Court of Canada and the decisions of such court(s) shall be binding on all parties.

12. This Agreement may be executed in one or more counterparts, each of which shall be deemed an original, but which together shall constitute the same instrument. Each of the parties acknowledges receipt of a copy of this Agreement, duly signed by each of the other parties and acknowledges that, through its directors and officers, it has read this Agreement, understands it, has had the opportunity to obtain independent legal advice about it prior to executing this Agreement, and agrees to its terms. If signed by an electronic signature, each of the parties agrees to be bound by its own electronic signature and to accept the electronic signature of the other parties.

IN WITNESS WHEREOF, each of the parties has caused this Agreement to be executed by its duly authorized representative.

[NAME OF PRODUCER]   [NAME OF COMPANY 1]

By: _____   By: _____
    Name: Name:
    Title: Title:

I have authority to bind the Corporation.   I have authority to bind the Corporation.

[NAME OF COMPANY 2]   [OTHER COMPANIES IF APPLICABLE]

By: _____
    Name:
    Title:

I have the authority to bind the Corporation.

[End of this sample agreement.]

NONDISCLOSURE and NON-CIRCUMVENTION AGREEMENT
MULTIPLE PARTIES (MUTUAL, MULTI-LATERAL)

This NonDisclosure and Non-Circumvention Agreement ("Agreement") is entered into as of [DATE] between:

[NAME OF PRODUCER] ("Producer"), a corporation incorporated under the laws of [INCORPORATING JURISDICTION], having its principal office at [ADDRESS];
and
[NAME OF OTHER PARTY 1] ("Company 1"), a corporation incorporated under the laws of [INCORPORATING JURISDICTION], having its principal office at [ADDRESS];
and
[NAME OF OTHER PARTY 2] ("Company 2"), a corporation incorporated under the laws of [INCORPORATING JURISDICTION], having its principal office at [ADDRESS]. [Any number of additional parties may be added]

Recitals

A)   The Producer, Company 1 and Company 2 [AND OTHER PARTIES IF APPLICABLE] (the parties other than the Producer being referred to collectively as the "Companies") are entering into discussions concerning the following production project: [SHORT DESCRIPTION OF PROJECT] (the "Project") for the purpose of determining whether the Producer and one or more of the Companies will enter into one or more agreements (a "Service Contract") for the provision by one or more of the Companies of services (the "Services") in connection with the Project;

B)   It will be necessary for each of the parties to disclose Confidential Information (as defined below) to one or more of the other parties during such discussions and, if a Service Contract is entered into for the Project by two or more of the parties, further disclosures of Confidential Information will be required;

C)   It is essential to each of the parties that all Confidential Information disclosed by any of them to one or more of the other parties be kept strictly and absolutely confidential and the parties have therefore agreed to enter into this agreement (the "Agreement") with respect to the Confidential Information; and

D)   The parties wish to ensure that their agreed arrangements regarding the receipt of commissions, fees, remunerations or other considerations to which they are entitled as a result of their involvement in the Project are not circumvented by one or more of the parties entering into arrangements with third parties;

Consideration

In consideration of the disclosures to be made by each party to one or more of the other parties, their mutual agreements set out in this Agreement and other good and valuable consideration, the receipt and sufficiency of which is expressly acknowledged by each of the parties, each of the parties covenants and agrees with all of the other parties as follows:

Definition of Confidential Information

1. As used in this Agreement, "Confidential Information" means any and all information and material concerning or relating to the party disclosing such information and material (the "Disclosing Party") and/or the Project (whether prepared by the Disclosing Party, or otherwise) that is furnished to one or more of the other parties (each of the parties receiving such information being referred to as the "Receiving Party"), orally, in writing, or electronically or in any other manner by or on behalf of the Disclosing Party and any material, information or work developed, derived or resulting therefrom, including, without limitation, summaries, notes, books, stories, scripts, proposals for film or television productions, names and/or descriptions of characters, marketing, and project development plans, technical information, business, and financial data, intellectual property of any nature, website designs, internet marketing or sales practices or strategies, and records of any type containing or otherwise reflecting such information or material.

Each of the parties acknowledges that "Confidential Information" does not include:

(a) information or material already known to the Receiving Party or in its possession, without obligation to keep it confidential, at the time of its receipt from the Disclosing Party;
(b) information or material received by the Receiving Party in good faith from a third party lawfully in possession of it;
(c) information publicly known at the time of its receipt by the Receiving Party or which has become publicly known through methods other than by a breach of this Agreement or other action by the Receiving Party or any of its directors, officers, employees, contractors or other representatives (the "Receiving Party's Representatives"); or
(d) information or material independently developed by the Receiving Party without reference to the Confidential Information for purposes other than the Project and/or the provision of the Services and without violating this Agreement.

Confidentiality and Non-Disclosure Obligations

2. The Receiving Party shall hold in confidence and use the Confidential Information solely for the purpose of participating in discussions with the other parties concerning the Project, including developing proposals for the Services to be provided by the Re-

ceiving Party, and carrying out its obligations if a Service Contract is entered into, and for no other purpose whatsoever. The Receiving Party shall not, during the continuance of this Agreement or at any time thereafter, without the prior written authorization of the Disclosing Party, (i) disclose any of the Disclosing Party's Confidential Information to any person other than the Receiving Party's Representatives or the representatives of another party to this Agreement who require such information for the purposes of participating in the discussions relating to the Project or providing Services, or (ii) copy, reproduce or release, directly or in any form, any Confidential Information or any work derived or resulting therefrom.

3. The parties acknowledge that none of them are under any obligation to enter into a Service Contract with the Producer or any other party and that any of them may terminate their discussions at any time and for any reason prior to the entering into of a Service Contract. Each Receiving Party agrees to return promptly to the Disclosing Party or destroy (subject only to the Receiving Party's legal obligations to retain records required for tax or other financial purposes) any copies, including all derivations, of Confidential Information in written or other tangible form upon request of the Disclosing Party or once the use of such information, to the limited extent permitted by this Agreement, is complete or upon termination of the Receiving Party's discussions without the execution of a Service Contract.

4. Each Receiving Party shall cause each of its affiliated, subsidiary and associated corporations and the Receiving Party's Representatives to comply with the Receiving Party's obligations under this Agreement and shall be fully responsible and liable to the Disclosing Party for any and all breaches of or failures to comply with this Agreement by one or more of such corporations and/or the Receiving Party's Representatives, whether or not the Receiving Party had knowledge of such breach or non-compliance.

5. Each of the parties acknowledges that its obligations under this Agreement with regard to the Confidential Information shall continue in effect after the execution of a Service Contract.

6. If any party commits a default or breach of its obligations under this Agreement (the "Defaulting Party"), the party or parties claiming to be damaged by such breach shall be entitled to terminate all discussions with the Defaulting Party immediately by written notice to the Defaulting Party and initiate proceedings to recover all reasonable costs (including legal expenses) incurred in enforcing or protecting its rights under this Agreement. Any such action shall not terminate this Agreement.

7. Each Receiving Party acknowledges that any breach of the covenants contained in this Agreement may cause the Disclosing Party irreparable harm, and remedies at law for any such breach may be inadequate. Accordingly, the Disclosing Party shall

be entitled to seek to obtain a restraining order, injunction, or another similar remedy (without any requirement to post a bond as a condition of such relief) for any breach or threatened breach of this Agreement by one or more Receiving Parties. Nothing contained in this Agreement shall be construed as limiting any party's right to any other remedies at law, including the recovery of damages for breach of this Agreement.

Non-Circumvention Agreement

8. Each of the parties agrees it will not attempt to circumvent the terms of this Agreement, or any Service Contract entered into in connection with the Project, in an attempt to gain commissions, fees, remunerations, or considerations for its benefit while excluding or depriving the Producer or another Company of the benefits to which one or more of such parties is entitled. Each of the parties further agrees that it will not, directly or indirectly through the use of or cooperation with any other person, firm or corporation, including an affiliate, subsidiary or associated corporation or a partner, contractor, subcontractor or other entity, enter into any agreement or another arrangement that could result in any such circumvention.

9. In the event that any of the Companies breaches or fails to honour its obligations under this non-circumvention agreement, each of the parties authorizes the Producer to initiate legal proceedings, on behalf of itself and the other companies which have suffered or may suffer damage as a result of such circumvention, to prevent and/or stop such circumvention and recover compensation for such damages. In the event that the Producer incurs legal expenses and/or other costs for the purpose of enforcing the rights of the parties under this non-circumvention agreement, each of the Companies acknowledges and agrees that the Producer shall be entitled to recover its costs, including without limitation its reasonable legal expenses, prior to damages recovered through the judgment of a court or a settlement, or in any other manner, being distributed to any of the parties.

General Provisions

10. None of the parties may assign this Agreement without the prior written consent of each of the other parties. Subject to that restriction, this Agreement shall be binding upon and inure to the benefit of the parties and their respective successors and permitted assigns. A waiver by any party of any breach by any other party of any of the terms, provisions or conditions of this Agreement or the acquiescence of a party in any act (whether of commission or omission) which but for such acquiescence would be a breach as aforesaid, shall not constitute a general waiver of such term, provision or condition for any subsequent act contrary thereto.

11. This Agreement and the Service Contracts (if and when executed) represent the

entire understanding between the parties with respect to the subject matter of this Agreement and supersede all prior written or oral agreements made by or on behalf of the parties with respect to such subject matter. Any amendment or modification to this Agreement must be in writing and signed by all of the parties.

12. If any provision of this Agreement is declared invalid by a court of competent jurisdiction, such provision shall be ineffective only to the extent of such invalidity, so that the remainder of that provision and all remaining provisions of this Agreement will continue in full force and effect.

13. This Agreement, the relationship of the parties, and any disputes relating to this Agreement shall be governed by and construed and interpreted in accordance with the laws of the Province of Ontario and the federal laws of Canada applicable in that province. Any action or proceeding to this Agreement shall be instituted in an Ontario court, or, if within its exclusive jurisdiction, the Federal Court of Canada and the decisions of such court(s) shall be binding on all parties.

14. This Agreement may be executed in one or more counterparts, each of which shall be deemed an original but which together shall constitute the same instrument. Each of the parties acknowledges receipt of a copy of this Agreement, duly signed by each of the other parties and acknowledges that, through its directors and officers, it has read this Agreement, understands it, has had the opportunity to obtain independent legal advice about it prior to executing this Agreement, and agrees to its terms. If signed by an electronic signature, each of the parties agrees to be bound by its own electronic signature and to accept the electronic signature of the other parties.

IN WITNESS WHEREOF, each of the parties has caused this Agreement to be executed by its duly authorized representative.

[NAME OF PRODUCER]

By: _____

   Name:
   Title:

I have authority to bind the Corporation.

[NAME OF COMPANY 2]

By: _____

   Name:
   Title:

I have the authority to bind the corporation.

[NAME OF COMPANY 1]

By: _____

   Name:
   Title:

I have authority to bind the Corporation.

[OTHER PARTIES IF APPLICABLE]

Chapter 7
IN SEARCH OF THE MONEY

Introduction

Well, you have a property to develop, you have completed the necessary agreements and registrations, and next it is time to prepare for the market. But how?

Now it is time to look for money: partners, investors, studios and, in general, anyone who might be interested in being part of your show.

You may have heard that the next step in doing this is to create a bible and/or a teaser to attract investment. Let's see why and what steps are needed.

The Bible

This is basically a pitch document that is used to present the idea. It is a compilation of different elements of the production.

The **bible** has certain elements that any reader will expect to find. They are:

- **Target audience.** We have to define who our audience is. For example, is it family-oriented, preschool, six-to-eight-year-olds, over 35, etc.?
- **Format and episode length.** Describe the number of episodes and the duration of each one.
- **Logline, also known as "elevator pitch," describing the show.** Describe in a line, in 20 seconds, in a nutshell what the show is all about.
- **Short line describing the type of style of the show.** Is it a comedy, drama, etc.? I always find it useful when creators create an analogy with another show; for example, this series is a mix of *Show A* and *Show B* with added elements of comedy. A table of show types is provided at the end of this section of the chapter.
- **Description (brief) of the idea's universe.** What are the guts of the story, where does it happen, etc.? We need to respond to the "five W's": who, what, where, when, why, as well as how.
- **Characters:** Describe them from head to toe; use visual references to the actor you wish to play the part or to a drawing; describe them not only physically but their personalities, characteristics, and traits.
- **Set the stage.** Where is the action happening, is it in the real world or a fantasy world?

Add some description of the places where the action is going to happen, add pictures or drawings.

- **Sample episodes.** A short synopsis of four or six episodes, no longer than four or five lines.
- **Sample script.** This is not a must, but some studios or broadcasters will ask you for it.
- **Brief bio.** This is not a must, but some studios or broadcasters will ask you for it.
- **Copyright line.**
- **Contact information.** Containing all the necessary details. You want to be sure that they can contact you anytime. Add your address, email, phone, WhatsApp, Skype, etc.

Table of Show Types

Action	Foreign	Reality
Adult	Gay	Religious
Anthropology	Game show	Romance
Animation	Health/Fitness	Science
Archeology	History	Sci-fi
Arts	Hobbies/How-to	Paranormal
Automotive	Home/Garden	Seasonal
Aviation	Horror	Shock value
Business	Hunting	Short
Children (4–6)	Inspirational	Soap opera
Children (6–8)	Interstitial	Sports
Children (6–12)	Lifestyle	Suspense
Comedy	Martial arts	Teen (12–19)
Cooking/Food	Men	Travel
Crime	Military	Urban
Current Affairs/News	Motor sports	War
Educational	Parenting	Western
Extreme Sports	Performance	Wildlife/Nature
Family	Period piece	Wine
Fantasy	Pets	Women
Fashion	Pre-school (up to 4 years)	Youth (7–12)
Film Noir	Psychological/Social	

The Teaser

In many cases, the bible is accompanied by a visual component that will help to convey in an accessible way the basic elements of the property. This is what is called a **teaser**.

A teaser is made before a movie/series is shot; the final objective is to "tease" the audience. Usually, the audience consists of other professionals with whom you would like to work on your movie, television program, video game or similar project, or it is meant to attract investors or to intrigue the public about an upcoming release coming soon to their screens. The teaser is made at the beginning of the project and is short in length, from 30 seconds to a minute—just enough to give the other party a little taste of what to expect.

Some people like to call this item a **trailer**, a **promo**, or a **pilot**, but a teaser is not the same as these other items. Although they are all for promotional and investment purposes, they are each completed during different steps of the production and in different parts of the sales process.

A **trailer** is made once the movie is completed, and it is a short, edited taste of what the movie promises to be, usually with some credits attached. It is mainly meant for exhibitors to play in their cinemas to show the viewer what is coming soon to their screens. In other words, it is a commercial advertisement for a movie. Trailers are now shown before the film begins at the beginning of the pre-launch campaign. They build up anticipation in the spectators.

A **promo** is anything that uses material from a movie to promote that movie. It can be presented in different ways such as behind-the-scenes interviews, featurettes, etc.

All these selling tools must "start fast" and "end big," i.e. begin with an enticing image and finish with a big explosion or something huge. The last scene must leave an impression and stay in the mind of the viewer. Do not edit in a linear way where one action follows another. In constructing a trailer we might put a scene from the end at the beginning or something from the middle of the show at the end. Basically, do not think linearly; tweak the three-act structure, which divides a story into three parts (acts), the **setup**, the **confrontation** or **development**, and the **resolution**. Above all, remember that audiences are more sophisticated now.

If the studio has given you the green light to make a **pilot**, you should be delighted as this a serious step when taken by a studio. A pilot usually is one episode of a series. Just one, where we can see the characters in motion, the action, etc. It is generally presented to a panel of spectators as a test to see their reactions. After these pitching sessions, normally they are asked questions about the show, their thoughts, the possibility of them becoming a loyal viewer, etc.

A Test

There are many cases, especially in animation, when you might want to check out the animation studio before assigning them the project to test their ability to convey the ideas, the quality of animation, their production schedule, and so on. Many animation studios charge a minimum fee for this, or in some cases they do it for free if you guarantee that they will be hired to do the work for the whole production (movie/series/etc.) provided that the test is successful.

Agreement for a Test Sample

AGREEMENT FOR TEST

The undersigned acknowledges the receipt of the script, character designs, props, backgrounds, and English dialogue track ("Materials") from the Producer of the series _____ for the purpose of evaluating the undersigned as a potential co-producer/subcontractor/service provider to the Producer with respect to any animated project, without present or future economic compensation of any kind, even in the event that the undersigned is not selected as the co-producer/subcontractor/service provider to the Producer. The undersigned further acknowledges that such Materials are confidential and are the exclusive property of the Producer, that the test will be the exclusive property of the Producer, and that the undersigned will not have any rights in such test work or the property itself. The length of the pilot shall be no less than 30 seconds.

The undersigned shall provide a test work (the "Test"), including, without limitation, all animation production from storyboard (including any extra designs) to compositing with editing, including retakes, delivered by secured FTP, and provided by the undersigned in High Definition 1920x1080 progressive. The undersigned will deliver to the Producer any and all work and files used and/or related to the production of such Tests.

The undersigned shall deliver the Test within one (1) month from receipt of the Materials.

The undersigned represents and warrants that it has no intention to use the Materials for its own benefit, or to disclose the Materials to any other person(s) or entity or to use it for the studio promotion of services or for any other purpose, except the production of the Test. The Material will be delivered without any watermarks or logos of the studios. The undersigned covenants and agrees that neither the undersigned nor any of its employees or agents will use for its or his/her own benefit or for the benefit or any person or any entity other than the Producer or disclose to any person or entity other than the Producer, any Materials. By accepting such Materials hereunder, the undersigned agrees that it shall keep the Materials with complete secrecy and confidentiality and that it shall not use the Materials for any purpose other than the production of the Test without the express, prior, written permission of an authorized official of the Producer. The undersigned further agrees to return all Materials to the Producer upon completion of the above-referenced evaluation.

Nothing in this agreement shall be deemed or construed to grant to the undersigned a license to use, sell, develop, or use as a demo, material in the demo tape/web or by any distribution method, exploit, copy or further develop any Materials, except for the purpose of delivering the Test. Furthermore, nothing contained in this agreement will be deemed to constitute a partnership between the Producer and the undersigned and neither of them will do, permit or suffer from being done, anything whereby it may be represented that one is a partner of the other or has the authority to make or give any commitment on behalf of the other.

The undersigned agrees that the laws of Canada shall govern this document, the relationship of the parties hereunder, and the resolution of disputes hereunder or relating thereto. Any action relating to this agreement shall be instituted in an Ontario court, or if within its exclusive jurisdiction, the Federal Court of Canada.

ACCEPTED AND AGREED:

By:(company) _____ Company Seal_____

Position & representative's name: _____

Company details _____

Place & Date: _____

Chapter 8
CO-PRODUCTIONS

Introduction

These days more often than before, especially in Canada, **co-production** is considered the best way to produce programs. But why is that? Let's go back a couple of steps and reflect on a simple question: How many people does it take to make a film? "Many," you would say. And that is true unless we are talking about a one-person project or independent films in some cases. But why do we need so many professionals? Simply because specialized people make better films. For example, to produce a movie, we require professionals who are masters in their various specialties to help us produce the best movie we can make. In an interview, Spanish director Pedro Almodóvar, was asked: "How can you produce such solid and beautiful movies?" His reply was clear: "I surround myself with the best professionals in each aspect of the production, no matter who they are or where they come from."

International Co-productions

International co-productions are film and television productions that are produced by two or more countries, such as the production of a recording, theatrical work, television program, etc. jointly with one or more producers. In official co-productions, the responsibility is shared between the co-producers.

Co-productions have been facilitated by international treaties, and these treaties allow the concerned parties to pool their resources and obtain national production status in their respective countries. Please take note that there can also be Canadian co-productions, either interprovincial when two or more Canadian production companies, from different provinces, decide to work together in a co-production, or within a single province, when two or more production companies in that province enter into a co-production agreement.

Each party brings particular strengths or contributions to the project.

Co-production, like anything else, has benefits and drawbacks. Benefits include:
- The ability to pool financial resources. If you can split the cost of the production with another party, the chances of making it happen are higher.
- Access to more sources of financing.
- Access to the partner's government's incentives and subsidies. Many countries around

the world have subsidies, tax credits, funds, and grants that the local producer can apply for. The objectives of these are to help producers pool the funds needed for production.

- Access to the partner's market, or to a third market. If the show qualifies as a national production of the co-producer's country, you can exploit the broadcasting quotas of that country. Broadcasting quotas have been established in many countries and refer to the minimum number of hours of programming a broadcasting company must use to air productions from its own country. Quotas are imposed by the government to protect and strengthen their country's local production industry. Thus, if the production counts as a national production of a certain country, it is more likely to receive airtime in that country, due to broadcasting quotas requiring the broadcast of local productions
- Access to a project initiated by a partner. It might be you or maybe another producer who has an idea for a production. The option of going into co-production allows you to work on the ideas of another producer.
- Access to a location or cultural benefits. Producing with another partner will give you access to locations in their territory and will provide you with great access to the cultural aspects of that country.
- The opportunity to learn from your partner. No two production companies produce content in the same way, even if the final objective is the same. Your co-producer may have a different structure, or you may choose a partner to be your co-producer because you consider them to be the best at what they will be contributing to the production.

Drawbacks of co-productions include:

- Increased coordination and production costs. This may happen if there are not clear stages of production processing or, as is called in the industry, **pipeline**; this can also produce delays in the production schedules with potential added expenses and subsequent budget increases.
- Increased costs associated with dealing with the government. Yes, applying for all the tax incentives, funds, grants, etc. has a cost that must be borne by the producer.
- Loss of control and cultural specificity. Sometimes there are some local cultural aspects that we do not want to have reflected in the movie, and that may be difficult to control.
- Time zone challenges. It is very often that the parties involved in the co-production reside in different time zones. In many cases, this may be a problem in terms of communication and productivity.

Basic Elements in any Co-production Agreement

The co-production agreement must include everything that has been agreed to between the parties because the agreement will supersede any prior discussions between those involved. There are some elements that are a vital part of co-production agreements. These include:

- Identification of the parties entering into the agreement (the co-producers) by their legal names.
- The effective date of the agreement and a statement that there is consideration exchanged between the parties (which may be in their respective agreements).
- Reference to the applicable International Co-production Agreement ("treaty"). You must ensure that the treaty specified in your agreement covers the medium of your project. You must determine which treaty will apply because normally only one treaty and some amendments will apply between the co-producers' respective countries. However, it may be the case that a country has separate treaties for different types of productions, such as movies, TV series, animation, etc. In that case you must verify that the treaty you are using reflects the kind of show that will be produced.
- Specifications of the Canadian and foreign producers' respective contributions to financing. Some rules must be followed in the agreement when describing these contributions, including describing the financial participation in the currency of the co-production country and in Canadian dollars; the exchange rates used must also be specified.
- A description of the percentage of participation of each producer in the total budget.
- The Canadian and foreign producers' respective copyright ownership rights, including ownership of the original negative or digital master. The agreement should also specify what will happen to copyright ownership should the co-production fail.
- A description of the respective distribution and exploitation rights of the Canadian and foreign producers.
- Specifications of how worldwide revenues will be shared.
- The due date for finalizing the long-form co-production agreement, if any.
- Many treaties also have specific requirements that must be included in your co-production agreement. See the following link for a list of conditions for the treaty you wish to use: http://www.telefilm.ca.

Some Key Aspects of Canadian Co-productions

Telefilm Canada is a federal Canadian cultural agency and on behalf of the Minister of Canadian Heritage it administers Canada's official co-production treaties that develop and promote

Canada's audio-visual industry, and acts on behalf of the Minister in evaluating applications for co-production certification. The final decision to allow or prohibit a project is made by Telefilm in Canada and the respective foreign authority.

The certification process involves two steps: advance ruling and final approval.

In the case of live action, the applications must be submitted at least 30 days before commencing production.

Some basic elements for certification are:

- The Canadian company must be controlled by Canadians per the *Investment Canada Act* as defined in the *Income Tax Act (Canada)*.
- To be an official co-production, the agreement has to be signed with a producer of a country that has an international co-production agreement with Canada or a memorandum of understanding; in the event of multiple co-production it must have a co-production deal with one of the other countries.
- The Canadian co-producer cannot be affiliated, associated, or be part of the foreign co-producing entity.
- The Canadian co-producer must keep all the exploitation and distribution rights for its own country and a share of the revenues from all other territories based on its investment. Associated with this, remember that the financial contribution of each party is equal to the share in the copyright.

Telefilm Canada will certify a program following these criteria:

- The producer has to be Canadian.
- The production must earn at least six out of 10 points in relationship to the key creative roles being performed by Canadians, i.e. the director, screenwriter, or one of the two lead performers must be Canadian citizens.
- A minimum of 75 percent of the production's service costs must be paid to Canadians.
- A minimum of 75 percent of the post-production and laboratory costs have to be completed in Canada by Canadians or Canadian companies.

A related item of interest to check is the CRTC *Canadian Program Certification Guide*.

The Commission also certifies that foreign programs must be dubbed in an official language of Canada or a native Canadian language.

When a production is certified as Canadian, it is assigned a certification number: a "C" number for any domestic Canadian production or the dubbing of a Canadian production; an "SR" number (special recognition) for an international co-venture or co-production; or a "D" number for the dubbing of a foreign production. As part of the certification, the time credit and category ("genre") will also be confirmed.[8]

The Canadian Audio-visual Certification Office (CAVCO) is responsible for certifying all independently-produced co-ventures, domestic productions, and dubbings of Canadian and foreign programs that are intended for broadcast as Canadian programming by a licensed Canadian broadcaster undertaking the production for the purpose of its Canadian program exhibition requirements.

According to the CRTC's guide,[9] the following types of productions are not eligible for certification as Canadian programs: infomercials, promotional and corporate videos/films, and other forms of advertising material, pornography, or projects containing a defamatory, obscene, or otherwise illegal nature based on the *Criminal Code of Canada*; repackaged or adapted versions of existing foreign productions or program segments, which use some or all the following: excerpts from an original foreign production; a significant portion of the original foreign production in essentially unedited chunks; or the mention of the original foreign production in the credits.[9]

Fifty-six countries, although this list must be checked periodically with Telefilm Canada as it may vary, have audio-visual co-production treaties and memorandums of understanding with Canada.[9] They are: Algeria, Argentina, Australia, Austria, Belgium, Bosnia-Herzegovina, Brazil, Bulgaria, Chile, China, Colombia, Croatia, Cuba, Czech Republic, Denmark, Estonia, Finland, France, Germany, Greece, Hong Kong, Hungary, Iceland, India, Ireland, Israel, Italy, Japan, Jordan, Korea, Latvia, Luxembourg, Malta, Mexico, Montenegro, Morocco, Netherlands, New Zealand, North Macedonia, Norway, Philippines, Poland, Romania, Russian Federation, Senegal, Serbia, Singapore, Slovakia, Slovenia, South Africa, Spain, Sweden, Switzerland, United Kingdom, Uruguay, and Venezuela.

The United States is not a party that currently shares a co-production treaty with Canada.

European countries tend to comprise most of Canada's co-production activity.

For co-productions, there are some incentives available such as access to private and public funding, Canadian federal content tax Credits, and provincial Canadian content or services tax credits. Since the production will be Canadian, there will be enhanced Canadian broadcast license fees.

These are some terms to take into consideration:

---

8. Guide to the CRTC Canadian Program Certification https://crtc.gc.ca/canrec/eng/guide1.htm
9. The number of countries with agreements with Canada according to Telefilm Canada's Website as of July 1, 2020. Please visit Telefilm's website to confirm or update the number of countries.

- The approving authority is CAVCO upon recommendation by Telefilm Canada.
- The Canadian co-producers must own the necessary rights to produce and exploit the co-production.
- Participation of the co-producers: normally, the minimum contribution and expenditure from any party in an international co-production is usually 20 percent of the budget (this percentage varies across countries; in some places the minimum may be as much as 30 percent and in one specific case, 15 percent, which is the minimum in China).
- The participation of both in technical and creative aspects has to be proportionate to the financial contribution of each party.
- The expenditures and copyright ownership must be as described in the co-production treaty.
- Only if allowed by Telefilm, and if required by the script, can you can shoot in a third-party country.
- The Canadian co-producer must retain all the rights regarding the distribution of the program in Canada and all Canadian exploitation rights.[10]
- Regarding the CAVCO points: if the co-production involves a European Union (EU) member country, the citizens of any EU country may qualify for points.
- Only the Canadian and foreign co-producers may get producer credits.

Key Personnel

Telefilm has identified the following persons as "key personnel" for the purposes of their analysis:[11]

For live action productions:

Director

Scriptwriter(s)

1st lead performer (based on on-screen time)

2nd lead performer (based on on-screen time)

Director of photography

Production designer/Art director

Picture editor

10. Comparison of Canadian Content, Production Services, Co-Ventures and Treaty Co-Productions (https://www.dentons.com/en/insights/articles/2015/march/31/comparison-of-canadian-content-production-services-co-ventures-and-treaty-co-productions).
11. International Treaty Co-Productions With Canada: An Overview For Producers (http://www.mondaq.com/canada/x/218474/Sport/International+Treaty+CoProductionsWwith+Canada+An+Overview+For+Producers).

Music composer

For 2-D animated productions:
Director
Scriptwriter(s)
Storyboard supervisor
Design supervisor/Art director
1st lead voice actor (based on on-screen time)
2nd lead voice actor (based on on-screen time)
Picture editor
Music composer

For 3-D animated productions:
Director
Scriptwriter(s)
Storyboard supervisor
Design supervisor/Art director
Character model supervisor
Motion capture supervisor
Animation director
1st lead voice actor (based on on-screen time)
2nd lead voice actor (based on on-screen time)
Picture editor
Music composer

The following participation by third-country performers is allowed by Telefilm:

Feature Films/Movies of the Week (MOWs):[12]
1 performer + 1 cameo (3 shooting days maximum)

12. http://tviv.org/Movie_of_the_week: A movie of the week (sometimes shortened to MOW or MOTW) is any movie—be it made-for-television or theatrical—which airs weekly in a timeslot reserved by a network for that type of programming. However, in Hollywood industry jargon, it refers to almost any movie produced by a broadcast network (or some non-premium cable networks, particularly those which rely heavily on ad revenues) specifically for distribution and debut on television and on that network. https://screennovascotia.com/starring-your-property/: MOWs are generally the same as features except budgets are often smaller. Cast and crew sizes are approximately 50-75.

Television Series:

Up to 6 episodes: 1 lead performer + 1 cameo OR 1 guest star;

7–13 episodes: 1 lead performer + 2 cameos OR 1 lead performer + 1 cameo + 1 lead performer OR 1 lead performer + 2 guest stars;

14–26 episodes: 1 lead performer + 4 cameos OR 1 lead performer + 2 cameos + 2 guest stars OR 1 lead performer + 4 guest stars.

"Cameo" means the brief appearance of an internationally known personality from a third-party country, involving no more than three shooting days, and "guest star" means the participation of a third-party country performer in one or more episodes of a series, according to the ratio set out above.

Telefilm Approval

Including the marketing material, Telefilm must approve the credits to be used in the exploitation of the production in all territories.

Courtesy Credits

In November 2010, Telefilm set out permitted exceptions to the rule that no third country producer-related credits will be allowed. Certain third country courtesy credits are now allowed, provided that, if a third country individual is given credit under Group A below, then at least one Canadian or co-producing country individual must be given credit from Group A as well. The same applies to Group B credits: for every third country individual accorded a credit from Group B, a matching number (or more) of Group B credits must be granted to Canadians or co-producing country individuals.

Group A:
Executive Producer
Senior Executive
Executive in Charge of Production
Supervising Producer
Associate Producer

Group B:
Supervising Executive

Production Supervisor
Production Executive
Production Associate
Executive Consultant
Production Consultant
Creative Consultant

Co-ventures

Co-ventures are another way of co-producing, but there are some specific rules and regulations. When it comes to co-ventures, the Canadian Radio-Television and Telecommunications Commission ("CRTC") is the approving authority.

An audio-visual project produced as a co-venture may:
- Access the Film or Video Production Services Tax Credit (PSTC).
- Be recognized as Canadian content for broadcast quotas and thereby benefit from more substantial broadcast licenses.

To be recognized as a co-venture, an audio-visual project must:
- Be produced by a Canadian company and one or more foreign companies;
- The Canadian company must: have financial participation varying between 50 percent (projects with francophone or Commonwealth countries or with which Canada has a co-production agreement) and 75 percent (projects with all other countries).
- The Canadian company must retain between 50 percent and 75 percent (according to the above cases) of the project's operating revenue.
- The director or screenwriter or main actor must be Canadian.
- The Canadian co-venturer must have sole or co-signing authority over the production bank account and the payment of the Canadian elements.
- Creative control must be shared equally between the Canadian and the non-Canadian party.
- Regarding the expenditure requirements: 75 percent of all service costs (below the line costs) must be paid to Canadians. The following costs are excluded from the 75 percent calculation:
    o Remuneration for producer(s) and co-producer(s) (except for producer-related positions);
    o Amounts paid to key creative personnel eligible for points;
    o Post-production costs;

- - Amounts paid in respect to accounting fees, legal fees, insurance, and financing costs;
    - Indirect expenses;
    - Contingency costs.
- 75 percent of all post-production/lab costs must be paid for services provided in Canada by Canadians or Canadian companies.
- If the co-venture is with a country which is part of the Commonwealth, French-speaking, or has a co-production treaty with Canada, the expenditure requirements are reduced to 50% for both services and post-production work.
- The production must achieve at least six out of 10 points for Canadian personnel. This requirement is the same as seen previously for Canadian content productions. A certain number of key roles must be occupied by Canadians on the same basis as for a Canadian content production, subject to one exception: If the co-venture is with a country which is part of the Commonwealth, French-speaking or has a co-production treaty with Canada, the points test is reduced to five out of 10. The director or the screenwriter and at least one of the two lead performers must be Canadian.
- The Canadian co-venturer must receive at least 50 percent of the share of profits from the exploitation of the co-venture.
- The Canadian producer is not required to retain all Canadian exploitation rights.
- The Canadian company is not required to hold the copyright on the project.
- There is no requirement that either of the parties has developed the production. However, one of them must own the underlying rights necessary to produce and exploit the production.
- Producer credits are not limited to the Canadian co-venturer. Producer credits should be balanced between Canadian and non-Canadian producers.
- A non-Canadian producer can have related credits (i.e. executive producer, associate producer, etc.).
- There is no restriction on granting courtesy credits.

Canadian Content

While talking about co-productions and co-ventures, several key elements need to be present. We see how we must create our co-partnership in such a way that the product can access a series of tax initiatives, enhance the broadcaster fees, and achieve other benefits. But there is another aspect that we must be aware of, and that is to know when a Canadian production qualifies as Canadian content:

- Incentives are available such as access to private and public funding, federal Canadian content tax credits, and provincial Canadian content or services tax credits. Since the production will be Canadian, there will be enhanced Canadian Broadcast License Fees.
- The approving authority is CAVCO upon the recommendation of Telefilm Canada.
- A Canadian producer must develop the production.
- The Canadian producers must produce the project and have financial control as well as creative control.
- In terms of the spending requirements, 75 percent of all service costs (generally, below the line costs) must be paid to Canadians.
- The following costs are excluded from the 75 percent calculation:
    - Costs determined by reference to the amount of income from the production;
    - Remuneration for producer(s) and co-producer(s) (except for producer-related positions);
    - Amounts paid to key creative personnel eligible for points;
    - Post-production costs;
    - Amounts paid in respect to accounting fees, legal fees, insurance, and financing costs.
- 75 percent of all post-production/lab costs must be paid for services provided in Canada by Canadians or Canadian companies.
- The Canadian producer must have all Canadian exploitation rights.
- The production must achieve at least six out of 10 points for Canadian personnel.
- Either the director or the screenwriter, and either one of the two lead performers, must be Canadian citizens but can reside outside of Canada or be permanent residents.
- No points will be allotted for a Canadian who shares the functions of a key creative position with a non-Canadian.
- For the lead performer, CAVCO looks at remuneration (including perks), credit, and screen time in making this determination.
- To obtain the points for the position of screenwriter, each individual involved in the preparation of the screenplay for the production must be Canadian. This means that all the individuals engaged in developing the screenplay from the outline or treatment through drafts, polish, to the final shooting script, must be Canadian.

- All positions related to the producer function must be held by Canadians unless there is an exemption.
- Exemptions for a foreign courtesy credit are granted by CAVCO. Note that no exemption will be granted for the functions of producer, co-producer, line producer or production manager, as these positions must be held by Canadians.
- Non-Canadians granted a producer-related screen credit (other than producer or co-producer, which is not allowed under any circumstances) are limited to being on set for a maximum of 25 percent of principal photography (other than for a lead performer, or an individual working in the story department, or a showrunner, who may be on set for more than 25 percent).
- An exemption for a foreign courtesy credit for non-Canadians not providing services may be granted by CAVCO only where the functions do not interfere with the financial and creative authority of the Canadian producer and relate to broadcast, distribution or financing, or the provision of services under the script supervision and control of the Canadian producer. An affidavit to this effect must be submitted.
- A non-Canadian showrunner must submit a non-Canadian showrunner affidavit declaring that any work performed is done under the direction and control and with the full knowledge of the Canadian producer.
- The Canadian producer must retain a fair share of revenues from the exploitation of the production outside of Canada.

To obtain more information on Canadian regulations in terms of Canadian content, please consult the following website: Canadian Radio-Television and Telecommunications Commission (CRTC) (crtc.gc.ca).

Co-production Sample Agreement

The following sample agreement, like all the others in this book, is just that—an example of what a co-production agreement might look like. Each contract must be carefully drafted to reflect your specific transaction and to ensure that it is complete. It is prudent to obtain legal advice from an experienced lawyer before entering into any legal agreement.

CO-PRODUCTION AGREEMENT FOR [Show title]

This Agreement is made on_____this_____day of_____20__

BETWEEN: [Canadian producer's company name], a company incorporated under the laws of Canada, whose registered office is at _____, Canada, represented by _____ as _____.

Hereafter referred to as "_____" and/or the **"Canadian Co-Producer."**
OF THE FIRST PART

AND: _____a company incorporated under the laws of _____, whose registered office is at _____ (_____), _____, represented by_____ as_____.

Hereafter referred to as "_____" and/or the "_____**Co-Producer"**

OF THE SECOND PART

WHEREAS, _____ and _____ (hereafter collectively referred to as the **"Co-Producers"**) intend to co-produce a _____ work provisionally or definitively entitled "_____" (**"the Series"**), having a running time of approximately_____ minutes with _____episodes, based on a script (or a book) written by_____;

WHEREAS, the **Co-Producers** have agreed to co-produce The Show in accordance with the provision of the bilateral agreement executed between _____ and Canada on Film Co-Productions dated _____ (hereinafter referred to as the **"Co-Production Treaty"**).

WHEREAS, the **Co-Producers** intend to produce and distribute the Series on the terms and conditions set out herein.

NOW, THEREFORE, in consideration of the premises and their mutual covenants and agreements herein contained, the Co-producers agree with each other as follows:

1. INTERPRETATION

1.1 Terms and conditions set out in this agreement or in any Schedule hereto which are usual in the industry in Canada and_____shall be interpreted in accordance with customary industry practices unless the context otherwise requires or the parties otherwise explicitly agree in writing.

1.2 The division of this Agreement into Articles and Sections and the insertion of headings are for the convenience of reference only and shall not affect the construction or interpretation of this Agreement.

1.3 Unless the context requires otherwise, words importing the singular include the plural and vice versa and words importing gender include all genders.

1.4 Unless the context requires otherwise, references in this Agreement to Articles, Sections, or Schedules are to Articles, Sections, or Schedules of this Agreement.

2. CO-PRODUCTION

2.1 The Co-producers agree as follows:

(i) to co-produce the Series in accordance with the terms of the present Agreement;

(ii) to exploit and distribute the Series worldwide, in its original version or any and all other versions, dubbed or subtitled, in all available known or yet to be known media, in accordance with the terms hereof;

(iii) to share all revenues, as provided hereunder, to be gained from the exploitation and distribution of the Series and;

(iv) to carry out their respective responsibilities and contributions as set out in this Agreement.

2.2 The Agreement shall not be construed as or constitute a partnership or an association between the Co-Producers other than for the purpose of the production of the Series as provided herein and no party hereto shall be entitled to act on behalf of any other party hereto and, in particular, no party shall be entitled to enter into binding obligations on behalf of any other party hereto.

2.3 All decisions relating to co-production, (including, without limitation, casting, key creative, crew, or replacements for any person, which shall be subject to the written approval by the parties hereto), financing, budget, distribution, pre-production, production, post-production, artistic production, editorial control and delivery of the Series shall be made after good faith consultation. In the event of any conflict that cannot be resolved by good faith discussion, each party shall have the final say on its part of the work. The parties shall, from time to time, set out in Schedules to this Agreement signed by each of the parties, their respective responsibilities relating to the carrying out of co-production decisions made after the effective date of this agreement. Such Schedules, once completed and signed, shall form part of this agreement.

2.4 Each party undertakes to exercise its rights granted in the Agreement so as not to cause a breach of any of its or the other party's obligations to third parties.

2.5 A teaser (hereinafter referred to as "**the Teaser**") will be produced to obtain financing for the production of the Series. The parties will work together to obtain development money for the production of such a Teaser. In this connection, _____ shall produce a 1-minute Teaser based upon a screenplay provided by _____. _____ shall provide _____ and _____ for the Teaser, once the development money is in place. In the event that a Teaser has already been produced prior to the signing of this Agreement, the rights in it will be shared in proportionate percentages equal to the respective co-production percentages of each of the parties as set out in this Agreement.

2.6 _____ agrees to produce a website based on the Series. The development, production cost, and maintaining of this website will be _____'s sole responsibility as will be agreed upon in a website co-production agreement to be entered into by the parties.

2.7 _____ and ____ agree to co-produce a webcasting version based on the Series. The respective responsibilities of the parties for the development, production cost, and maintenance of this webcasting proposal site will be agreed upon in a webcasting co-production contract.

3. BUDGET & FINANCING

3.1 It is the intention of the parties to obtain financing for the production of the Series. The parties intend that the production budget for the Picture will be CAD$__M(millions), which is equivalent to_____. The conversion rate used is _____CAD$ The parties acknowledge that __% of the production budget for the Series will be producers' fees which shall be split between them in the same proportions as their agreed percentage of ownership in the copyright between _____ and _____. A detailed production budget (hereinafter referred to as "**the Budget**") will be attached to this Agreement. In the event that the parties are successful in attracting production funds or if they agree in writing to produce the Series by themselves without external assistance, then the parties will produce the Series in accordance with the terms herein. The parties shall have mutual approval of the terms of any financing agreement ("Production Financing Agreement") with any third party. The parties agree that, at a minimum, the terms of any Production Financing Agreement will include the provision that all costs of production and delivery of the Series, including fees and interest, if any ("Negative Costs") are to be repaid from the Gross Revenues, as defined below. Notwithstanding the foregoing, _____ shall be primarily responsible for _____ of the Series and _____ shall be primarily responsible for the _____ for the Series.

The parties agree that the Budget shall be sufficient to cover the full cost of production and delivery of the Series to all third parties and distributors.

3.2 The Series shall be produced in accordance with the Budget for the Series. Any material change in the Budget shall require the prior written approval of each of the parties.

3.3 The cash flow of each party's financing shall be agreed upon between the Co-Producers as per the approved budget, and the parties shall consult with each other in good faith regarding the approval of the budget and any changes to it.

3.4 Any budget overages approved in writing by all Co-Producers shall be borne by the parties in proportion to their respective percentage contributions to the Budget. For any overages not so approved, each Co-Producer shall be solely responsible for any such overages incurred in connection with the elements which it is providing (unless such overage was caused by a default on the part of the other party, in which case, such other party would be responsible for the overage) and for greater certainty, responsibility for such overages shall not affect their respective agreed upon contributions.

3.5 Additional co-producers and co-financiers shall be entitled to be mentioned in the credits of the Series and, where relevant, in the copyright ownership line of the Series, as set out in Article 11 below.

3.6 Other than as expressly set out herein, no party to this Agreement may assign or transfer, in any manner, any of its rights and/or obligations under this Agreement without the prior written consent of the other Co-Producer(s) or contracting parties.

3.7 Details of any permitted assignment/transfer (including any credit obligations granted to third parties) pursuant to Article 3.5 and/or 3.6 above shall be made known to the other party within thirty (30) days of execution of the assignment or transfer agreement.

4. SERIES SPECIFICATIONS

4.1 The Series shall have the following specifications:
Provisional or definitive title: _____ (English Title)
Original Language: English
Director: TBA
Created by: TBA
Screenwriters: TBA
Produced by: _____ & _____

Voices:	TBA
Original songs and music:	TBA
Running Time:	___minutes x ____episodes
Material:	_____

4.2 The Co-producers may make changes to the above specifications at any time in accordance with the procedures set out in Article 2.3.

4.3 All other specifications of the Series, including but not limited to character design, storyboard, animation supervision, coloring, layout, editing and compositing, accounting personnel, etc. shall be decided by the Co-Producer responsible for that specific portion of work according to the Budget and after meaningful consultation with the other Co-Producer and final approval by _____. However, _____ will have final full artistic, production, and editorial control for the Series.

4.4 Each of the Co-Producers hereby acknowledges receipt of the chain of title documentation.

4.5 Subject always to the rights of any possible financing agreements or additional co-production agreements for the Series, _____ hereby transfers and assigns ___ percent (__%) of all and any rights included and not limited to authors rights, underlying rights, moral rights, residuals, merchandising, copyright, trademark, industrial rights, license rights, incidental and ancillary rights and all and any present and future rights whether now known or hereafter devised regarding the property (such rights hereinafter collectively referred to as "**the Rights**" and/or "the Property") to _____ so that the parties shall jointly own the Series and its property rights and copyright in the following percentages:

_____ % (__ percent)

_____ % (__ percent)

4.6 Subject to the provisions above, the period of the assignment shall commence on the date of signature of this Agreement and continue in perpetuity whether or not the Series is produced.

5. ACCOUNTING

5.1 The Co-Producers shall keep each other fully informed about the progress of production and post-production of the Series.

5.2 Each of the parties shall maintain specific books of accounts to record and register all their respective expenses incurred during the pre-production, production, and post-production.

5.3 Each party and its accountants shall be granted access to the books of accounts of the other party with respect to the Co-Production during reasonable business hours, upon providing the other party with at least forty eight (48) hours prior notice. Any such access shall be carried out without unnecessary interference with or disruption of the normal conduct of the business of the other party.

5.4 Each of the parties shall, within 90 days after the acceptance of the first print made from original camera negatives or answer print, provide to the other party a financial report giving the final and definitive cost of the portion of the Co-Production for which it is responsible for accounting hereunder. This report shall be in a form similar to the Budget for the Co-Production, which has been accepted and agreed upon by the parties.

5.5 ____ **Canadian Account** - A special bank account will be opened at the _____ Bank, _____address_____, Canada, Account #: _____, Swift: _____, IBAN Number: _____ from which payments are to be made of all Canadian expenses of the Co-Production.

5.6 ____ **Account** - A special bank account will be opened in the United Kingdom at the _____ Bank, _____address_____, England, Account #: _____, Swift: _____, IBAN Number:_____, from which payments are to be made of all UK expenses of the Co-Production. The parties may also operate a cashing facility in or near the production location in Scotland.

6. THIRD PARTY CONTRACTS

6.1 The benefit of all contracts concluded by one Co-producer in relation to the production of the Series shall be deemed held by that party for itself and the other parties.

6.2 None of the Co-Producers shall enter into any contract nor permit any third party to enter into any contract which:

(i) Contains terms which might result in the Budget being exceeded save as set out in this Agreement or as otherwise agreed to in writing by the other Co-Producer(s);

(ii) Grant to third parties any rights in the negative of the Series, digital master or any part thereof in the Series or the Screenplay without the prior written approval of both co-producers.

7. INSURANCE

7.1 The production insurance provided for in the Budget shall be in full force for all risks prior to the commencement of the animation of the Series and shall insure against those customary events usually considered in standard insurance policies of the motion picture industry such as:

(i) Loss, damage or destruction of the negative and other related image and sound elements of the Series;

(ii) The risk of accident, illness or death of the director including the risk of abandonment resulting from such accident, illness or death;

(iii) Public liability covering injury to third parties and/or damage to property;

(iv) Employer's liability; and

(v) Liability for errors and omissions in the chain of title to the Co-production, infringement of copyright for defamation, or invasion of privacy.

7.2 Each insurance policy shall have the Co-Producers (and any other financial partners as the Co-Producers shall reasonably require) named as insured for its respective interest. Certified copies of all policies shall be sent to the other Co-producers promptly after signature and in any event no later than the commencement of the animation of the Series.

7.3 Each party shall notify the others on the happening of any event which may give rise to a claim under any insurance policy. Each party shall consult with the others about the settlement of any insured losses.

7.4 The premiums for such policies shall be paid out of and included in the Budget of the Series. The policies shall be kept in force and effect until the Series has been completed and delivered. No revision, modifications or cancellation of such policies shall be made by any party without first obtaining the prior written approval of the other Co-Producers.

7.5 Each party agrees that it will not do or permit to be done anything which may cause any such insurance policy to lapse or become wholly or partly void or voidable by the insurers.

8. DELIVERY

8.1 All original sound and image negatives and other materials relating to the Series shall be kept at one or more laboratories selected by _____ (hereinafter referred to as "**the Laboratory**").

8.2 The Co-Producer responsible for the post-production of the Series shall notify the others in writing (hereinafter referred to as "**the Notice of Availability**") that the following initial materials (hereinafter referred to as "**the Initial Materials**") are available at the Laboratory:

(i) A digital hard drive of the original version of the Series and Trailer;
(ii) A video master in a format to be determined by the Co-Producers of the Series and Trailer;
(iii) Music & Effects (M&E) tracks of the Series and Trailer; and
(iv) Text-less titles for the Series;

8.3 Each of the Co-Producers shall be entitled to receive all materials necessary for the distribution of the Series, including:

(i)   A dialogue list of the original version of the Series and Trailer;
(ii)   Press Kit including stills;
(iii)   Original poster design;
(iv)   A Certificate of Origin of the Series;
(v)   Music Cue Sheet; and
(vi)   Full list of billing and credit obligations.

9. DISTRIBUTION AND TERRITORIES

9.1 The parties will have exclusive distribution rights in the following territories, save and except those rights in the territory of the other Co-Producer.

PNC: Canada and _____
together with all military installations, ships, and aircraft flying flags of the above-mentioned territories.

_____: (Its own territory) and_____

together with all military installations, ships, and aircraft flying flags of the above-mentioned territories.

9.2 The revenues and expenses for each territory shall be distributed among all media and markets in that territory but not between that territory and another territory.

9.3 The parties would have the right to appoint sales agents in its own territories with a distribution fee no higher than 30% of the gross revenues.

9.4 The parties shall each have access to the others and third parties' publicity material(s) with respect to the Co-production.

9.5 All prints and all printed material used in the distribution and exploitation of the Co-production shall include the following:

A Country 1 & Country 2 Co-Production

A mention of the Co-production companies and their respective individual producers shall also be made.

10. RECOUPMENT AND PROFIT PARTICIPATION

10.1 Recoupment of the parties' financial contributions to the Budget and profit participation shall take place as set out in this Article.

10.2 All revenues earned from the exploitation of the Series shall be deemed "Gross Revenues" and shall be distributed as follows: (a) firstly, towards the commission and distribution expenses, (b) to the repayment of the Negative Costs in accordance with the terms of any Production Financing Agreement(s), as contemplated under Article 3 hereof, (c) 50% (or less if negotiated by the parties) of the Net Revenues to the financiers pursuant to any Production Financing Agreement (d) the balance of the Net Revenues shall be divided _____ by _____ and _____. "Net Revenues" shall be defined as the Gross Revenues less the commission and distribution expenses and the Negative Costs. The parties shall have the right to grant a percentage of the Net Revenues to third party investors, broadcasters, talent, etc. All decisions on the number of Net Revenues to grant to third parties shall be subject to the mutual approval of the parties.

10.3 In the event the Series is produced, the parties intend to license experienced third parties to organize the licensing and merchandising of all products based upon the Property and the Series, which will include, without limitation, clothing (including children's clothes, nighttime apparel, adult clothes, etc.), games, video games, computer software, linens, posters, furniture, books, comics, calendars, party goods, toys, plush toys (including, without limitation, dolls and puppets), gadgets, cosmetics, food, beverages or other similar products or novelties commonly considered as "merchandising" items (hereinafter referred to as "**Merchandised**

Products"). All revenues generated from the merchandising and licensing of the Merchandised Products shall be referred to herein as the "Merchandising Revenues." The Merchandising Revenues shall be considered part of the Gross Revenues. The terms of the agreement(s) for the licensing of Merchandised Products shall be subject to the mutual approvals of the parties, not to be unreasonably withheld or delayed. Furthermore, the terms of this paragraph shall be subject to the terms of the Production Financing Agreement to the extent that such agreement provides for the licensing of Merchandised Products.

11. OWNERSHIP OF RIGHTS IN THE SERIES

11.1 As far as the Rights are concerned, the copyright in the Series and the Property shall be jointly owned by the parties in the following proportions:

_____   __% (__ percent)
_____   __% (__ percent)

11.2 The copyright notice for the Series and all and any property related to the underlying rights shall be as follows (subject to the rights of other Co-Producers and financiers):

If abbreviated notice: ©&TM (Year). _____ Entertainment Inc. and _____. All Rights Reserved.
If short notice: ©&TM (Year). _____ Entertainment Inc. and _____

11.3 The parties shall be entitled to add further copyright owners to the copyright ownership line of the Series only as provided in this Agreement or subsequently agreed by the parties in writing.

11.4 The negative and all other physical materials of the Series shall be in the ownership of the parties in the following proportions:

_____   __% (__ percent)
_____   __% (__ percent)

12. CREDIT PROVISIONS

12.1 Each of the parties shall be granted corporate and one or more individual "co-producer" credits in the main titles on all positive prints of the Series and in all paid advertising (subject to customary exclusions) to be agreed upon by all Co-Producers.

12.2 The parties agree that there shall be accorded in the Series such credits as the parties shall be obliged to accord in their contractual arrangements with third parties (including, but not limited to, their financiers), subject to such credits being in standard industry form.

12.3 The parties shall contractually require that all credit entitlements in respect to the Series are respected by all third parties, including individuals and companies distributing or exhibiting the Series, but shall not be held liable for any default thereof. The parties shall, as soon as reasonably practicable, make reasonable efforts to remedy any such default of which they receive written notice but not so as to oblige the parties to incur any legal costs or other substantial expenses.

13. **TERM AND TERMINATION**

13.1 The term of this Agreement ("the Term") shall commence as of the date hereof and shall expire three years from the date the Teaser is delivered to the parties unless, prior to such a date, the parties enter into a Production Financing Agreement, in which case this Agreement shall continue without time limit. The copyright of the property, the underlying rights, Teaser and Series, shall be owned ___% by _____ and __% by _____ in perpetuity, whether the Series is produced or not.

13.2 If any party (i) commits a material breach of its obligations under this Agreement, and (ii) the other party gives written notice to the defaulting party specifying the breach, and (iii) if the breach is capable of being remedied but is still not remedied fourteen (14) days after the date of receipt of said notice, then the party giving the notice shall be entitled to terminate this Agreement by written notice to the defaulting party.

13.3 If an Event of Insolvency occurs in relation to a party, then, with respect to that party, the other parties shall be entitled to terminate this Agreement by written notice. "Event of Insolvency" shall mean any deterioration in the financial circumstances of a company which prejudices the ability of the company to fulfill its financial obligations.

13.4 Upon termination in accordance with this Article, the defaulting party's interest in the Screenplay, the Series, the Property, the physical materials of the Series, and the money in production accounts relating to the Series shall, so far as legally permissible, automatically terminate and be transferred to the other parties in shares proportionate to their percentage interest in the Co-Production. For this purpose, the defaulting party shall execute all confirmatory documents reasonably required by the other parties.

14. **FORCE MAJEURE**

14.1 An event of *force majeure* shall mean a failure to perform any obligation hereunder caused by any fire, earthquake, flood, extreme weather condition, epidemic, accident, explosion, casualty, strike, lockout, riot, civil disturbance, act of a public enemy (including terrorists or paramilitary organizations), embargo, war, act of God, any municipal or state ordinance or law, any legally constituted authority, whether municipal or state, or by the issuance of any executive or judicial order or any other event beyond the reasonable control of the party required to perform.

14.2 Any failure by either party to perform any obligation hereunder resulting from an event of "*force majeure*" occurring prior to completion of the production of the Series shall not be deemed to constitute a breach but, if such failure continues for more than one (1) month, this Agreement may be terminated by any party (by giving written notice to the other parties), with such termination being effective ten (10) days from the receipt of such notice. In the event that this Agreement is so terminated, the party not claiming *force majeure* shall be entitled to substitute a third party of its choice.

14.2. An event of *force majeure* shall mean a failure to perform any obligation hereunder caused by any fire, earthquake, flood, extreme weather condition, epidemic, accident, explosion, casualty, strike, lockout, riot, civil disturbance, act of public enemy (including terrorist or paramilitary organizations), embargo, war, act of God, any municipal or state ordinance or law, any legally constituted authority, whether municipal or state or by the issuance of any executive or judicial order or any other event beyond the reasonable control of the party required to perform. This definition must stay as it is a standard legal form!!!!

15. APPLICABLE LAW AND JURISDICTION

15.1 In the event of any dispute, claim, question, or difference arising out of or relating to this Agreement or the breach thereof, the parties shall use their best endeavours to settle such disputes, claims, questions, or differences. To this effect, they shall consult and negotiate with each other, in good faith and understanding of their mutual interests, to reach a just and equitable solution satisfactory to all parties promptly upon notice by any party specifying full particulars of the dispute and, if they do not reach such solution within thirty (30) days thereafter, then either party may deliver written notice to the other party requiring resolution, at the choice of the party bringing the complaint, either by independent arbitration or through the judicial process, and thereafter refer the dispute, claim, question or difference in issue to arbitration for final settlement binding on all parties in accordance with the provisions of the commercial arbitration legislation applicable in the venue in which the party instituting legal proceedings is resident.

15.2 It is agreed that each party shall be entitled to translate the terms of this Agreement into its own language and have the other parties execute such translations if so required by the relevant national authorities. Notwithstanding the execution of any such translations, the parties agree that in the event of any conflict between the terms of such translations and the terms hereof, this English language form of the agreement will prevail and be legally valid and binding between them.

16. NOTICES

All notices, statements, service of process or other documents which either party shall be required or shall desire to give to the other party shall be in writing and shall be given by either (a) personal delivery, or (b) first class registered post with return receipt requested.

If so delivered or posted, each such notice, statement, or other document shall be conclusively deemed to have been given when personally delivered or on the date indicated on the return receipt as the case may be. Until further notice in writing, the addresses of the parties shall be:

To: _____
Attn:
CANADA
Phone:
Email:

To: _____
Attn: _____
(COUNTRY)
Phone:
Email:

17. GENERAL PROVISIONS

17.1 Nothing contained herein shall create any association, partnership, joint venture or the relationship of principal and agent between the parties, it being understood that the Co-Producers are, with respect to each other, independent contractors, and neither party shall have any authority to bind the other or the other's representatives in any way save as set out in this Agreement.

17.2 Each of the parties shall, at the request of the other, from time to time after the date hereof, execute and deliver such other instruments and documents, as may be reasonably necessary to further evidence, perfect, maintain, effectuate or defend any and all respective rights and obligations of the parties hereunder.

17.3 This Agreement constitutes the entire agreement between the parties hereto and supersedes all prior agreements and understandings, oral or written, by and between the parties hereto with respect to the subject matter hereof. No amendment, modification, supplement, change or waiver of the provisions of this Agreement shall be valid unless in writing signed by or on behalf of the parties hereto.

17.4 A party and any of its confidants will treat the confidential information confidentially and will not use or draw upon the confidential information other than for the purposes of this agreement and will not reproduce or copy in any fashion whatsoever in whole or in part the confidential information except as necessary for use as authorized in this agreement. The parties will ensure that it and its confidants do not disclose the confidential information to any other party. The confidential information will only be disclosed to the confidants of a party. For the purposes of this Agreement, "confidential information" includes all data and material furnished or disclosed by one party to the other directly or indirectly, in a tangible or intangible form, on or after the effective date of this agreement and so not as to restrict the generality of the foregoing, including, whether given in written format or orally, documentation, proprietary, private or restricted, technical or marketing information, product and customer information, specifications, characters, related backgrounds and props or the derivative works, including but not limited to rough drawings, clean-up drawings, illustrations, thumbnail sketches, storyboards, layouts, colours, model sheets, character profiles, models, samples, computer programs, software, firmware, all financial data, and information, all personnel or human resources-related data and information, and any and all information in relation to the business, customer and product strategies, plans, directions or projections of any of the parties. The parties shall not, during or after the period of such party's performance of the Services, disclose to any person or use for such party's own benefit or the benefit of anyone, nor allow the disclosure or use by anyone else, of such confidential information without the prior written consent of the other parties.

17.5 Notwithstanding the foregoing, the following information will not be deemed confidential:

a)   Information which at the time of disclosure is in the public domain;
b)   Any information of one party which, after disclosure, becomes part of the public domain by publication or otherwise through no fault of the other party or its Representatives or by a breach of this Agreement;
c)   Information which was lawfully and independently received by the party from a third party who was legally free to disclose the Information;
d)   Information which a Court of competent jurisdiction or governmental agency has directed, by final order, a party or a person to whom the party has furnished the Information, to disclose to others.

Information that is specific shall not be deemed to be in the public domain because it is embraced by general knowledge in the public domain. Further, the information shall not be deemed to be in the public domain merely because its individual features are within the public domain unless the combination of features or their nexus is in the public domain.

17.6 The parties will be free to perform consulting, co-productions, and other services for other clients and/or partners during the term of the Agreement; provided, however, that the parties ensure that they are able to perform in a timely manner all obligations deriving from the Agreement.

17.7 No party may assign this Agreement except in accordance with Article 3.6 and with the prior written consent of all other parties. Subject to the foregoing, this Agreement shall inure to the benefit of and be binding upon their respective parties hereto and their permitted successors and/or assigns. Any licenses granted with respect to rights under this agreement shall be subject to such terms and conditions of this Agreement are applicable thereto, and any party granting a license shall do so only in accordance with the Agreement and shall ensure that the license agreement incorporates all applicable terms to this Agreement.

18. APPLICATION TO NATIONAL AUTHORITIES

18.1 The parties shall co-produce the Series in compliance with the respective governmental approvals of Canada and _____ and subject to variations as each national authority may jointly approve from time to time.

18.2 Each **Co-Producer** with respect to their respective national authority shall be responsible for the submission of all relevant information in connection with the co-production of the Series pursuant to the **Co-Production Treaty** and for endeavouring to comply with any terms or conditions upon which any approvals by such national authorities have been or may be given.

18.3 Each **Co-Producer** shall register the **Series** and all relevant contracts with the relevant national authorities in its own country and shall, itself, bear the costs of such registration unless such costs are included in the **Budget**.

18.4 The parties expressly agree to hereby make reasonable efforts to have this Co-Production Agreement approved by the Competent National Authorities both in _____ and in Canada. In the event that, having obtained provisional approval and notwithstanding the parties best efforts, the **Series** is refused final approval as a co-production Series by the Competent National Authorities, the parties hereby agree that this Co-Production agreement shall remain, to the extent that is allowed by the applicable law, in full force and effect and each party shall remain liable for all sums undertaken to be advanced by it under this Co-Production Agreement.

18.5 The approval of the Co-Production by the competent Co-Production treaty authorities of either country shall not be interpreted as binding such authorities to grant any license of whatever kind to exhibit the Co-Production.

18.6 The following schedules are appended to this Agreement and are incorporated by reference and deemed to be part hereof:

SCHEDULE 1 – CHAIN OF TITLE
SCHEDULE 2 – BUDGET
SCHEDULE 3 – PRODUCTION SCHEDULES
SCHEDULE 4 – LABORATORY ACCESS LETTER

IN WITNESS WHEREOF, the parties have executed this Agreement on the date set out above.

By: _____   By: _____

By: _____   By: _____

SCHEDULE 1 – CHAIN OF TITLE
SCHEDULE 2 – BUDGET
SCHEDULE 3 – PRODUCTION SCHEDULES
SCHEDULE 4 - LABORATORY ACCESS LETTER

Chapter 9
BUDGET AND SCHEDULE

Budget

At the same time that we are creating our schedule and know the crew of professionals that are going to be involved, the **budget** is developed. Budgeting is an essential part of the filmmaking process. It includes all costs incurred in development, pre-production, production, post-production, and promotion. There are several basic elements that are part of the budget and that we must understand before we can create one:

First, there are two levels to a budget: the **summary** or **top sheet** and the **detailed budget**:

- **Summary or top sheet.** A synopsis of the budget, usually one or two pages in length. It is a summary of the detailed budget.
- **Detailed budget.** Lists every specific item needed to produce a show and its cost, in lines and columns. Both the summary and the detailed budgets have to match.

Second, budgets are divided into two main sections: **above-the-line** and **below-the-line**:

- **Above-the-line.** Here we establish the creative costs of the production that include rights payments, options, royalties, script fees, etc. and key creative talent associated with the production such as actors, producers, writers, etc.
- **Below-the-line.** Here we cover crew, equipment, subcontractors, etc. Basically, all other monies required to produce the project. These expenses are usually fixed. There is no associated creative aspect and, therefore, no options or royalties.

Third, **fringe benefits** in a budget represent the costs associated with salaries, such as union pensions, health and welfare contributions, employer matching contributions, employment insurance, taxes, etc. Normally these expenses are based on guild standards.

Fourth is the **bond fee** or **completion guarantee**, for production insurance purposes, provided by film insurance companies. It is usually between two percent (2%) and six percent (6%) of the total budget. It is used to guarantee that the producer will complete and deliver the movie, providing financiers, investors, etc. with peace of mind.

Fifth is **contingency**—a provision in case there are unexpected or unforeseen costs to guarantee completion and delivery on schedule. It is typically established at ten percent (10%) of the budget. In the rare event that the production of the movie is abandoned, the completion guarantor will repay in full all sums invested in the film by financiers.

Other important elements to keep in mind are:
- **Chart of accounts codes.** Code numbers are used to facilitate accounting and tracking of expenses for the accountants. To do that, each line, category, and any possible cost has to have a number code. For example, if the script section uses the code 0101, then each subsection will be numbered accordingly with the subsequent numbers.
- **Format.** The budget is divided into lines and columns. In the line, we place the name of the work, writer, for example. In the columns we put the following information: Chart of accounts code (code number); description of the position (description); salary amount for each individual in that work (amount); what is the unit of measurement, days, hours, (unit); how many people in that category (X); rate per job category (rate); subtotal and total.

There are different budget software products in the market that will help you to build your budget. Even though you can use Microsoft Excel to create your budgets, it is recommended that you use one of the specific budget programs to make things easier as all the items are already categorized. One of the most common programs is called Movie Magic. (See Appendix 2.)

Schedule

This must be divided into two main elements, the **general production schedule** and the **production board strips**:

1. The general production schedule provides the producer, investors, and participants with a broad view of the activities to be developed in the movie and how much time (usually in days) those activities will take. It helps with project execution and control. This document consists of several rows indicating the work to be developed: script, script editing, storyboards, storyboard revision, etc. In the columns are the months and days of the week which are used to determine how long each activity will take. See the sample *Santa versus Claus* (Appendix 3).

2. Production board strips. These are created by the Production Manager, and are used to organize the shooting schedule for the day. A production board strip will have as many rows and columns as needed for the following elements:

- Scene number (Scene #)
- Description of whether this is an interior or exterior scene (Int/Ext)
- Scene Heading, action description (Scene Heading)
- When the action is going to be shot, daytime or nighttime (Day/Night)
- What cast members need to be present (Cast)

- Place where shooting will occur (Shooting Location)
- Every page is divided into eight one-inch sections. This measurement is used to estimate the screen time and shooting time for a scene (Page Count)
- Estimated shoot time expressed in hours (Est. Shoot Time). It is estimated that you can shoot/record five pages per day with one page equal to one minute of screen time.

Production Board Strips

SCENE #	INT/EXT	SCENE HEADING	DAY/NIGHT	CAST	SHOOTING LOCATION	PAGE COUNT	EST. SHOOT TIME (HRS)

Chapter 10
INSURANCE

Introduction

When you are producing, many things can happen. A camera breaks, an actor gets sick, there are problems with the master, etc. As a producer, after investing so much money in the project, you need to be protected against any unexpected situation that might happen during the production, or even after the show is produced.

There are two types of insurance that a producer must obtain:
- **Entertainment insurance**, also known as **production insurance**.
- **Errors and omissions insurance**.

Types of Insurance

Entertainment insurance is designed to insure your property or the property of others in the production. It provides reimbursement for the losses and expenses incurred when a covered incident occurs. There is usually a deductible, which is an amount that is not reimbursable, intended to discourage small claims. A higher deductible will imply lower premiums because you're responsible for more costs before coverage starts.

The majority of producers choose to have an annual policy as that way they can reduce the premium cost and administration.

It is standard that the coverage provided by an entertainment insurance policy include:
- **Cast and animals insurance.** If a cast member cannot perform due to injury, sickness, or death, this insurance will cover losses resulting from interruptions in production and additional filming days. This also includes animals, which have to be accompanied by a qualified handler and have all their veterinarian certificates in order.
- **Negative film.** In case the negative film, raw film or tape stock, artwork, designs, drawings, computer software, and related material gets damaged, this policy will cover the extra costs necessary to complete the work.
- **Technical equipment.** Covers the equipment used in connection with your production, either owned or rented, if it is damaged or stolen. It is essential and is also called **replacement cost coverage**.

- **Sets and scenery.** This will cover loss or damage to wardrobe, costumes, sets, scenery, props, and other similar property.
- **Property.** Covers any damage caused by the production to property owned by third parties, such as studios, stages, commercial buildings, or residences.
- **Office equipment.** If it is stolen, lost, or damaged.
- **Extra costs.** Facilities or equipment being damaged or theft of equipment.
- **Production vehicles.** Loss or damage to the company vehicles during production.
- **General liability.** This covers expenses such as defence costs, legal fees, and other claims costs in a bodily injury or property damage case.

Errors and Omissions Insurance

This insurance can also be called **libel insurance**, **media perils**, or **media liability insurance**.

Every project is unique and therefore requires a unique, specific Errors and Omissions (E&O) policy. For example, the coverage required for a biographical movie is not the same as the coverage needed for an animated show for preschoolers.

Basically, this insurance is malpractice insurance for filmmakers. It covers legal liability and defense costs for the production company if it has to defend itself against lawsuits. Some policies also cover allegations of unfair competition and failure to provide screen credit. Among the elements of coverage are the following:

- **The right of privacy or publicity.** This will cover allegations that wrongful acts or omissions of the producer or others for whom the producer is responsible have infringed on a performer's right to control the use of his or her own identity for business or economic purposes, the performer's right to privacy when not in a public place, misleading or damaging information about the performer being publicly disclosed, or the details of his/her private life from becoming public information.
- **Infringement of copyright or trademark.** This will cover the defense of a court action alleging infringement of another person's copyright or trademark and payment of damages awarded to that person.
- **Libel, slander, defamation of character.** When a false statement is made publicly that damages another person's reputation, that is **defamation**. The statement constitutes **libel** when there is a permanent record of the defamation, such as a newspaper article, a radio or TV broadcast, a website posting, an email, or some other form of a written statement. **Slander** is an untrue oral defamatory statement of which there is no permanent record, such as a comment made to other people or even a derogatory gesture. A defamatory statement can

be made in any medium. Where a person is found to have been libeled, it is not necessary to prove quantifiable damages; it will be presumed by the court that damages were suffered. However, greater damages will be awarded if the libeled person can provide proof of actual damage suffered. In a slander suit, in order to be awarded damages, the person claiming to have been slandered must prove that he or she suffered quantifiable damages because of the false statement.

- **Plagiarism, piracy, or unfair competition.** The word "plagiarism" comes from the name Plagiarius, a kidnapper, and is the act of stealing or copying from the original source and failing to give credit to an author or creator. Piracy is the infringement of copyright.

Production financing will usually not flow until this insurance is in place. Once the producers fill out an application, they will receive a clearance report that will be used to obtain E&O insurance. Distributors in North America will not distribute a production without E&O insurance.

E&O Insurance can help pay for lawsuit expenses such as legal fees, court costs, and administrative costs and the damages paid as agreed in a settlement or as awarded by a court judgment.

This insurance does not cover:

- **Intentional wrongdoing or harm.** This is when you purposely do some kind of damage or injury to another person or property.
- **Illegal acts.** This describes actions that are not permissible according to law. These actions are forbidden and punishable by law.
- **General liabilities.** These are covered by what is often called **business liability** insurance, which covers you and your company for claims involving bodily injuries and property damage.
- **Employee injuries.** These are what we also call workers' injuries, when someone in the development of his/her work has an injury or experiences some kind of harm. Prevention and safe work practices help to avoid these kinds of injuries.
- **Employee lawsuits.** When someone who is working or worked for you sues you for any reason. The most common reasons are employment discrimination and wrongful termination, wage law violations (the employer violated a federal or provincial wage law), discrimination suits not based on employment, violation of a person's civil rights, and breach of contract.
- **Property damage.** This is property (public or private) that has been physically damaged by a person who is not its owner, or by natural phenomena.

In order to certify that E&O insurance has been obtained, the producer must obtain a **certificate of liability insurance**. Distributors and other parties that you are dealing with will request a copy of the certificate to confirm that your company has E&O insurance. The information provided on the certificate of liability insurance falls into the following categories:

- **General information about the production company and its insurers.** Lists who your insurers are and information about your company.
- **Coverage information.** Describes the nature of your insurance.
- **Description of operations.** Describes what your company does as a business—its activities.

A certificate of liability insurance can help to:

- **Secure contracts and clients.** In many cases, clients or potential customers require that you have insurance to do business with them. In fact, you should have insurance not only because they demand it, but because you as a producer need to be protected.
- **Provide clients with peace of mind.** As mentioned above, having insurance and being protected reassures clients of the viability of the project.

Different factors will affect the cost of this insurance, including:

- **Whether a lawyer's services were used** to secure clearances and licenses.
- **The coverage limits.** What is or is not covered in the insurance and the amount of the deductible.
- **Coverage territory**, i.e., local, national, international. Where are we covered? You have to be very specific regarding where you are covered. You usually want to be covered in any country where the production is taking place.
- **Type of distribution** and the distribution media: cinemas, TV, SVOD, etc.
- **Type of production and length.** What kind of production is this? A documentary? A TV series? Is this a one-off or a series of episodes?
- **The subject matter of the production.** What is the content of the production's storyline?
- **Production budget.** Insurance costs vary depending on the budget. Obtaining insurance for a low-budget project is not the same as obtaining insurance for a high-budget show.
- **Company's size, including the number of employees and annual revenues.** How many professionals are working with us? How much are they earning?
- **Business location.** City or town where your company carries out its activities.
- **Training and experience of your employees.** Qualification of the professionals working on the show.

- **Claims history** can affect premium costs as well, depending on how many claims you have previously submitted and their amounts.

Chapter 11
DISTRIBUTION

Introduction

There are many reasons why we produce a show, but I think that the two main ones are to artistically express our ideas to a broader audience and get our message across in the best way possible, and to make some money while doing it. Some people can make a living by doing this as a full-time job, and for that, it is essential that we obtain revenues from the exploitation of the property in different media. We are in the business of storytelling, but we also need to pay our bills. So, to be successful, we need to sell what we create, and there's an industry for that.

Technology has been evolving and changing rapidly in recent years, especially in the audiovisual industry. New media for content creation has been developing fast, as have the delivery methods, providing new ways of connecting and sharing with people that go further than traditional theatrical and television broadcasting. In the past, the process for a movie release was to have a theatrical exhibition first, then video or DVD, pay-per-view, pay-TV cable, and finally free TV. Another avenue was hotel and airline exhibition. Then video on demand (VOD) appeared, and things started to change. Now there are new computer programs accessible to many people to create content. Anyone can make their own movies using a cellphone as a video recording and editing device. At the same time, this new content gets rapidly shared on platforms such as social media. The traditional broadcasting system has been affected by the proliferation of companies like Amazon and Netflix.

When producers work on the finances of a show, they have to take distribution into consideration. **Distribution agreements** are often necessary for the completion of the finance plan for the production. **Distribution advances** are key in the financing process. This means that the distributor will commit to putting forward some funds towards the distribution rights while the show is still in production (and sometimes even before the commencement of production). Sometimes it is not possible to get an advance, but how, when, and where the show will be distributed, and how the distribution rights will be negotiated, need to be taken into consideration when we begin to plan our production.

When distributors give an advance, normally they want to have some say in the production, and they might require a schedule for approvals. Distributors want to make sure that the production will meet the original standards agreed upon regarding concept, creativity, and quality.

This is very reasonable if we understand the risk that the distributor is taking by investing in a product that is not yet finished (and sometimes not even started.)

There are very different distribution channels for film, TV, and the internet, and this means that different contract provisions will need to be included in the distribution agreement, depending on the media in which the production will be distributed.

And, by the way, if you are wondering—yes, the distributor will charge a fee for their work. This fee depends on the situation and the exhibition media. For example, for a theatrical release, the commission can be up to 50 percent of sales revenues. For TV, home video, and other types of media, it varies between 25 percent and 35 percent, with 35 percent being the most common. Distributing a show can get very expensive. The distribution company must attend many events to showcase their products, such as markets, festivals, and summits. They need to send representatives and salespeople, meet with the buyers, rent a booth so they can be seen, and create promotional materials such as bibles, flyers, and the always useful and collectible "goodies" to attract more people. They also advertise in industry magazines and may even organize cocktail parties for specific markets.

One of the biggest enemies of the producer and the distributor is **piracy**. Piracy is the illegal copying of copyrighted material with the objective of illegally selling it and obtaining a benefit. There is also internet piracy where whoever uploads a movie or a TV series receives no benefit or compensation other than to be able to allow others to stream it or download it for free

Distribution Agreements

A distribution agreement is a legally binding and enforceable agreement between the owner of the distribution rights of a film or video (the producer), and a company that is in the business of marketing and selling such works to users and purchasers (the distributor).

As we have seen with other agreements, there are some basic structural components and provisions that must be included in the agreement. These include:ion is a director or authorized signing officer of the corporation.

- **Parties to the agreement.** The parties to the agreement may be individuals or corporations. They must be identified by their correct legal names. If a corporation is a party, the other party's lawyer should verify that the corporation's name is shown correctly, that the corporation is in existence and has legal status to enter into an agreement in the jurisdiction where the agreement is being signed and that the person signing on behalf of the corporation is a director or authorized signing officer of the corporation.

- **Definitions.** Definitions of essential words and phrases that are being used in the agreement may be included to establish specific meanings for them that will apply when the agreement is being read and interpreted. For example, in the sample distribution agreement, "person" is defined as "any natural or legal entity." This means that when you read the word "person," it may be referring to either a corporation or a human being (or both). Definitions help to make the other agreement terms simpler and avoid repetition when the defined word or phrase is used more than once in the agreement. It is imperative to negotiate the wording of the definitions as part of the negotiation of the agreement to ensure they correctly reflect the parties' intentions. It is also very important to review the definitions carefully when you are reviewing an agreement provided to you by another party.
- **Granting of distribution rights.** The agreement will need to specify, in as much detail as possible, what rights are being granted, the payment terms, and the limitations on those rights. All commitments of the parties to each other must be included. Some examples of issues that will need to be covered are:
    o What rights are being granted, i.e., is it just for TV or for all media?
    o What will be paid or how will the parties determine how much is to be paid for granting those rights? Typically, there will be advances, guarantees, and/or royalties calculated as a percentage of the sales revenues.
    o For which territory are you granting the rights, i.e., the entire world, several specified countries, or just Canada?
    o How long is the license period (the term of the license), i.e., five years, 10 years? Will the license term be different for distribution through various forms of media?
    o Are the rights exclusive? If exclusive rights are granted, the distributor is the only one with the contractual right to sell the property or rights. If non-exclusive rights are granted, other distributors may be involved in the sales of the production. Usually, distributors ask for exclusivity.
    o Through what media is the distributor being licensed to distribute the production? The media are usually divided among theatrical and non-theatrical; home video, broadcast, and cablecast; SVOD and internet. Since some of these media overlap, the agreement should contain a definition of the scope of the media rights being granted.
    o "Reservation of rights" provision. This provides that all rights not explicitly granted to the distributor are reserved by the producer.
- **Who will pay for the distribution expenses?** Typically, it is the distributor, who is entitled to recoup them. The agreement should itemize the statements and supporting re-

ceipts and other information that the distributor must provide to the producer to confirm that the amounts being paid to the producer are correct. It should also state when and how frequently the statements are to be provided and payments made.

- Where a producer is being paid a percentage of income, the producer should have the right to **audit the sales**. Some agreements provide that if the audit discloses errors of more than 5 percent in the producer's favor, the distributor must pay the cost of the audit plus the amount owed to the producer.
- The distributor may want the right to **edit the show** without the producer's consent. The producer's concern will be how to ensure that the quality of the production is maintained and that the copyright and other underlying rights obtained by the producer permit editing.
- **Contractual commitments of the parties to each other.**
    - The distribution agreement will contain a list of materials the producer is required to provide to the distributor.
    - The distributor must guarantee to the producer that it will use its best efforts to promote and sell the property.
    - The producer must obtain a certificate of errors and omissions insurance (see Chapter 10).
- Each party will make **representations and warranties** to the other party. If a statement is false or misleading and, as a result, the other party suffers loss or damage, that other party has a contractual right to sue the party who made the statement, to recover compensation. For example, if the producer gives a representation and warranty that it has obtained the underlying rights needed for the distributor to distribute the product and that turns out not to be true, the distributor may be able to obtain a court judgment ordering the producer to compensate the distributor for its expenses and loss of profits. Also, if the distributor is sued by the wronged copyright holder, the producer may be liable for the distributor's costs of defending the legal proceeding and paying whatever damages are awarded. It is, therefore, essential to ensure that all statements made in the agreement are accurate and complete.
- **Default and termination provisions.** The agreement should set out the circumstances in which either party may terminate the agreement before its specified expiration date and what happens if a party fails to perform its obligations. For example a provision should be included in the agreement that would allow either party to terminate the agreement if the other party goes bankrupt. As well, if a party defaults in the performance of its contractual

obligations, the other party may have the right to terminate the agreement or to terminate some of the rights granted in the agreement. Depending on the nature of the default, the party claiming that there has been a default may be required to give the other party written notice of the default and the opportunity to correct it within a specified amount of time before the agreement can be terminated. There may also be performance requirements on the part of the distributor so that, if the distributor is not achieving the minimum targets, the producer can terminate the agreement and find a more effective distributor. The agreement may include dispute resolution provisions that specify how agreement disputes are to be resolved, i.e., by arbitration, by the courts, in which jurisdiction, etc.

- **Other provisions.** There will be some general provisions (sometimes referred to as **boilerplate provisions**), which are usually included in most types of agreements. They should be reviewed carefully. One such provision that should be noted will state that the provisions of the written agreement supersede all prior agreements, arrangements, and understandings between the parties, whether oral or in writing. If you have had discussions with the other party and reached verbal agreements on certain matters, or if you have prepared written summaries of the parties' preliminary agreements, such as a letter of intent, everything agreed to must be included in the agreement.

- **Good faith in performance of agreements.** In November 2014, the Supreme Court of Canada released a unanimous judgment in the case of Bhasin v. Hrynew 2014 SCC 71 [Bhasin]. It confirmed the legal principle that parties to a contract are under a duty to act honestly in the performance of their contractual obligations. The court stated that while parties remain free to negotiate the best deal they can and do not have to lay all their cards on the table or take the other party's interests into account, "a basic level of honest conduct is necessary to the proper functioning of commerce" [par. 60]. The court stressed that the principle "does not impose a duty of loyalty or of disclosure or require a party to forego advantages flowing from the contract; it is a simple requirement not to lie or mislead the other party about one's contractual performance" [par. 73] To date, this case had had less impact than many lawyers expected when the judgment was first released, but it is a reminder that being dishonest in your business dealings may jeopardize your ability to enforce your contractual rights.

International Standard Audiovisual Number (ISAN)

The **ISAN** "is a voluntary numbering system and metadata schema for the unique and persistent identification of any audiovisual works and versions thereof including films, shorts, documentaries, television programs, sports events, advertising, etc." Through the ISAN version, it is possible to identify all related versions of work such as variants (expressions, manifestations), language, editions, clips, media embodiments, digital encodings, etc. The ISAN version also allows for the identification of closely related content and items, including promotional material, soundtracks, closed captioning tracks, etc.

ISAN is not related to any form of copyright registration. It is basically a number given to a production and is typically placed in the end credits, or on any printed material relating to the show. It is like a barcode with a unique number that identifies a property, and in the case of a series, every episode has its own unique separate code.

DISTRIBUTION AGREEMENT

Dated: _____, 20__

Parties: _____ Distributor ("Distributor")
Canada

And _____ Producer ("Producer")
Country

This Agreement confirms the terms and conditions under which the Producer appoints the Distributor as the exclusive distributor of the Program (as that term is defined below) in accordance with the Particulars set out in section 2 of this Agreement and the other terms & conditions set out in this Agreement. In the event of any conflict between the Particulars and the other terms and conditions of this Agreement, the former shall prevail. All future cycles of the Program shall be subject to the terms and conditions of this Agreement unless otherwise agreed in writing by the Producer and the Distributor.

NOW, THEREFORE, in consideration of their respective covenants and agreements set out in this Agreement, the parties agree with each other as follows:

1. DEFINITIONS (in alphabetical order)
The following are the definitions to be used in interpreting this Agreement:

"Affiliate" means any Person (including any officer, director, employee, or partner of any Person) owned or controlled by, controlling or under common control with a Party.

With respect to any Person, Affiliate means any other Person directly or indirectly controlling, controlled by, or under common control with, such a Person. For the purpose of the foregoing, the expression "control" (including its correlative meanings, "controlled by" "controlling" and "under common control with") shall mean the possession, directly or indirectly, of the power to direct or cause the direction of the management and/or policies of such a Person; with respect to any natural person. Affiliates shall include, without limitation, such natural Person's spouse and family members.

"Airline" means any airline facilitating or permitting the exploitation of a Motion Film or Television Series Copy for direct exhibition in airplanes which are operated by an airline flying the flag of any country in the licensed territory for which Airline exploitation is granted, but excluding airlines which are customarily licensed from a location outside the licensed territory or that are only serviced in, but do not fly the flag of, a country in the licensed territory.

"Ancillary" means the right to exploit the Program for direct exhibition to passengers on Airlines, Ships, Buses, Trains and/or Hotels under the flag of any country of the Territory.

"Availability Date" means the first day after the end of the Holdback Period, or the period beginning on the Closing Date and ending on the anniversary of the Closing Date, for a Licensed Right. If the Availability Date refers to a category of Licensed Rights, it refers to the first date on which a Distributor may exploit any Licensed Right in the category.

"Broadcast" means the communication of a Motion Film or Television Series to the public by means of wire, cable, wireless diffusion, radio waves or by digital signals (whether synchronous or asynchronous) via a packet-switching communication system, that allows the Motion Film or Television Series to be accessed by the public and viewed on a television receiver. Broadcast means the same as telecast or diffusion. Unless otherwise set forth in the Deal or Agreement Terms, the number of broadcasts licensed under this Agreement shall be unlimited.

"Business Day" means a day other than a Saturday or Sunday or a day which is a public holiday in Toronto, Ontario, Canada.

"Cable–Free TV" means the originating transmission (whether analog, digital or otherwise) of a Motion Film or Television Series Copy by means of a coaxial or fiber-optic cable for reception on a television receiver in private accommodations without charge being made to the viewer for the privilege of viewing the Motion Film or Television Series. For the purposes of this definition, neither governmental television receiver assessments or taxes nor the regular periodic service charges (not a charge for Pay-

Per-View or Pay TV) paid by a subscriber to a cable television system will be deemed a charge to the viewer.

"Cable Pay TV" means transmission or retransmission of a Motion Film or Television Series Copy by means of an encoded signal (whether analog, digital or otherwise) over coaxial or fiber-optic cable for reception on a television receiver in private or temporary living accommodations by means of a decoding device where a charge is made: (i) to the viewer in private living accommodations for the right to use the decoding device for viewing any special channel which transmits the Motion Film or Television Series Copy along with other programming; or (ii) to the operator of a hotel or motel (or similar temporary living place), apartment complex, co-operative, condominium project or similar place located at a distance from the place where such broadcast signal originated for the right to use the decoding device to receive and retransmit the programming on such a channel throughout such places.

"Cassette" means the same as Videocassette.

"CDI" means the same as Compact Disc Interactive.

"Cinematic" means Theatrical, Non-Theatrical, and Public Video exploitation of a Motion Picture.

"Commercial Video" means the exploitation of a Motion Film or Television Series Copy embodied in any Videogram only for direct exhibition in a linear form before an audience by and at the facilities of either institutions or organizations not primarily engaged in the business of exhibiting Motion Films or Television Series, such as educational organizations, churches, restaurants, bars, clubs, trains, libraries, Red Cross facilities, oil rigs, and oil fields, or by and at the facilities of governmental bodies such as embassies, military bases, military vessels and other governmental bodies flying the flag of the licensed territory, but only to the extent that such exploitation is not otherwise utilized in the licensed territory as a form of Non-Theatrical exploitation. By way of clarification, Commercial Video does not include exploitation of the Film or Television Series by Theatrical, Public Video, Non-Theatrical, Airline, Ship, or Hotel exploitation.

"Compact Disc" means a combined optical and electronic storage device designed to be used in conjunction with a computer that causes a Motion Film or Television Series to be visible on the screen of a monitor or television receiver for viewing in a substantially linear manner. A Compact Disc does not include any type of Videocassette or Videodisc.

"Compact Disc Interactive" when used as a Licensed Right is a type of Interactive Multimedia Right and, when used to describe a Work, is a type of Interactive Multimedia Work.

"Cross-Collateralization" is the ability to make use of cash flow generated by one project to cover the expenses of a different project. Cross-Collateralization shall be limited to the Programs identified in this Agreement.

"DBS (Direct Broadcast Satellite)" means a form of broadcast in which the signal, encrypted or not, is transmitted by the sender via satellite, directly for a reception in individual homes without any intervening station, provided the recipient is in possession of the necessary equipment to receive the signals.

"Delivery" means delivery to the Distributor of the Delivery Materials, consisting of the Initial Materials and the Additional Materials, as provided in the Deal Terms attached as a Schedule to this Agreement.
"Digital Television (DTV)" means broadcast by a digital signal. A digital signal transmits the information for video and sound as ones and zeros instead of as a wave. For over-the-air broadcasting, DTV will generally use the UHF portion of the radio spectrum with a 6 MHz bandwidth, just like analog TV signals do.

"Disc" means the same as Videodisc.

"Distributor" means the party that is acquiring the Granted Rights from the Producer, pursuant to this Agreement, and its successors and permitted assigns, and to the extent provided in the applicable contract, includes the Distributor's approved and authorized agents, sub-agents and sub-distributors, and their successors and permitted assigns.

"Download" or "Downloading" means electronic digital transmission of a copy of the Program, which results in the creation of an electronic digital copy of the Program on the recipient's Licensed Device.

"DVB (Digital Video Broadcast)" means the broadcast of a Motion Film or Television Series Copy, stored in digital form on the server of a provider and such digital signal(s) to be transferred to the viewer/user's computing device (including but not limited to a mobile phone, Digital Video Broadcasting – Handheld (DVB-H), Digital Multimedia Broadcasting(DMB), etc. irrespective of the technology/system, the means by which signals are carried and whether a charge is made to the viewer/user or not, where the data material is (directly or after storage) decoded to make the Motion Film or Television Series Copy in a linear fashion visible on a screen of the viewer/user's computing device (including but not limited to a mobile phone). DVB shall include any form of exploitation via closed-circuit packet-switching communication systems but shall exclude the world wide web (www).

"DVD" means digital versatile discs (DVD) and is a type of Videodisc. DVD includes related DVD enabled peripherals such as DVD-ROM devices and DVD-RAM devices but does not include any type of Compact Disc.

"Exhibition" means the same as a public performance.

"Free TV" means all forms of Terrestrial Free TV, Cable Free TV, and Satellite Free TV exploitation of a Motion Film or Television Series. Free TV does not include any form of "pay-per-view" telecast or other exhibition not specified herein.

"Force Majeure" means any fire, flood, earthquake, or public disaster, strike, labour dispute or civil unrest, embargo, riot, war or insurrection, or any other Act of God.

"GAAP" means Generally Accepted Accounting Principles.

"Granted Rights" means all of the rights granted to the Distributor with respect to the Program pursuant to this Agreement, including but not limited to the rights granted pursuant to Article 2 of this Agreement.

"Gross Receipts" means the sum on a continuous basis of the following amounts derived with respect to each and every Licensed Right:

- All monies or other consideration of any kind (including all advances, guarantees, security deposits, awards, subsidies, and other allowances) received by, used by, or credited to the Distributor, any Distributor Affiliates or any approved sub-distributors or agents from the license, sale, lease, rental, lending, barter, distribution, diffusion, exhibition, performance, exercise or other exploitation of each of the Licensed Rights in the Picture, all without any deductions; and
- All monies or other consideration of any kind received by, used by, or credited to the Distributor or any Distributor Affiliates or any approved sub-distributors or agents as recoveries for the infringement of any Licensed Rights in the Picture; and
- All monies or other consideration of any kind received by, used by, or credited to the Distributor or any Distributor Affiliates or any approved sub-distributors or agents from any authorized dealing in trailers, posters, copies, stills, excerpts, advertising accessories or other materials used in connection with the exploitation of any Licensed Rights in the Picture or contained on Videograms embodying the Picture.

"High Definition" or **"HDTV"** means technology based on the following standards: Aspect ratio—16:9. Resolution—1920 x 1080 pixels. Frame rate—range from 24p (24 frames per second, progressive) to 60p (60 frames per second, progressive). Some of the commercial and public systems include, but are not limited to, consumer acquisition (HDV) and optical disc systems (HDDVD and Blu-ray).

"**Home Video**" means Home Video Rental and Home Video Sell Through exploitation of a Motion Film or Television Series.

"**Home Video Rental**" means the exploitation of a Motion Film or Television Series Copy embodied in any Videogram which is rented to the viewer for the sole purpose of a non-public viewing of the embodied Film or Television Series in a linear form in private living accommodations where no admission fee is charged with respect to such viewing. Home Video Rental does not include the public performance, diffusion, exhibition, or broadcast of any Videogram.

"**Home Video Sell Through**" means the exploitation of a Motion Film or Television Series Copy embodied in any Videogram which is sold to the viewer for the sole purpose of the non-public viewing of the embodied Film or Television Series in a linear form in private living accommodations where no admission fee is charged with respect to such viewing. Home Video Sell Through does not include the public performance, diffusion, exhibition, or broadcast of any Videogram.

"**Hotel**" means the exploitation of a Motion Film or Television Series Copy for direct exhibition in temporary or permanent living accommodations such as hotels, motels, apartment complexes, co-operatives or condominium projects by means of closed-circuit television systems where the telecast originates within or in the immediate vicinity of such living accommodations.

"**Intellectual Property Rights**" means any intellectual or industrial property rights throughout the world, including, without limitation:

(i)   the right to apply for (or submit an application for) a patent, trademark, service mark or design protection in any country or region, including the right to apply for such protection under any international treaty;
(ii)   the right to have a patent, trademark, service mark or design protection in any country or region registered or granted upon application;
(iii)   a registered or granted patent, trademark, service mark or design in any country or region;
(iv)   an unregistered trademark, service mark or design in any country or region;
(v)   copyright in any country or region;
(vi)   trade secrets, know-how, and confidential information;

and a license or other right to use or to grant the use of any of the foregoing, or to be the registered proprietor or user of any of the foregoing.

"**Interactive Multimedia**" means the exploitation of an Interactive Multimedia Work by means of a computing device that allows the Interactive Multimedia Work to be directly perceived and manipulated by the user of the computing device and that either stores the Interactive Multimedia Work on the user's computing device or accesses a Copy of the Interactive Multimedia Work by electronic means from another computing device interconnected with and located in the immediate vicinity of the user's computing device or by means of a one-way or two-way network.

"Interactive Multimedia Work" means a Work consisting primarily of a presentation communicated to a user through the combination of two or more mediums of expression, whether textual, audio, pictorial, graphical or audiovisual, where a significant characteristic of the presentation is the ability of the user to manipulate the content of the presentation by means of a computing device in real-time and in a non-linear fashion.

"Interactive Networked Multimedia" means the exploitation of an Interactive Multimedia Work over the facilities of a communications system that allows the user of a computing device to engage in two-way transmissions over the system to access the Interactive Multimedia Work, irrespective of the operator of the system or means by which signals are carried, and that stores a copy of the Interactive Multimedia Work for transmission over the system at a place distanced from the place where the user's computing device is located.

"Internet" means the open, world-wide, cross-platform network commonly known as the World Wide Web and/or any successor or alternative networks thereto (whether now known or hereafter devised) or any part thereof which may be accessed by the Hyper Text Transport Protocol suite and/or any successor or alternative protocols thereto (whether now known or hereafter devised).

"Internet Protocol Suite" (commonly known as **TCP/IP**) is the set of communications protocols used for the Internet and other similar networks. It is named from two of the most important protocols in it: The Transmission Control Protocol (TCP) and the Internet Protocol (IP), which were the first two networking protocols defined in this standard.

"Internet Protocol Television (IPTV)" is a system through which digital TV service is delivered using the architecture and networking methods of the Internet Protocol Suite over a packet-switched network infrastructure, e.g., the Internet and Broadband Internet access networks, instead of being delivered through traditional radio frequency, broadcast, satellite signal, and cable television (CATV) formats.

"Laser Disc" is a type of Videodisc.

"Law" means any statute or ordinance, whether municipal, provincial, state, national or territorial, any executive, administrative or judicial regulation, order judgment or decree, any treaty or international convention, or any rule, custom, or practice with force of law.

"**Licensed Device**" means any physical device capable of displaying, broadcasting, transmitting, or receiving Licensed Media in any form.

"**Licensed Media**" means the physical, electronic and other media of sale, rental, distribution, sub-distribution, broadcast or transmission in which or through which the Distributor is entitled to commercially exploit the Program in the Territory for the Term; in all languages throughout the territory during the Term to all media and in all formats and technical configurations whether now or hereafter known including but not limited to theatrical, SMS or any phone system, webTV, free television, cable television, pay cable television, subscription television, over-the-air pay television, closed circuit television, master antenna television, direct broadcast satellite television, video-on-demand, armed forces, in-flight use, video cassettes and video discs for home use, non-theatrical uses (including but not limited to educational institutions, clubs, hospitals, embassies and means of transport), broadband, mobile and wireless technology, all music rights, internet and e-commerce rights, merchandising (manufacture, distribution, sale and advertising in the Territories of merchandise articles of every type and description including but not limited to games and computer games) and publishing rights (including publication in electronic or other interactive form), or in translation, books and other publications based on or utilizing the Copyright or Trademarks.

"**Licensed Service**" means any service facilitating or permitting the display, broadcast, transmission, or reception of Licensed Media in any form.

"**Meaningful Consultation**" means, regarding the subject matter for which the right of Meaningful Consultation is granted, the procedure to be established between the Producer/Licensor and the Distributor under which (i) the Distributor will advise the Producer of decisions it proposes to make regarding the subject matter and (ii) the Distributor will provide the Producer with the relevant information reasonably requested by the Producer under the Distributor's control regarding the subject matter, and (iii) if the Producer objects to the Distributor's decision or course of action or requests that the Distributor consult further with the Producer regarding the subject matter to which the information relates, the Distributor will so consult and will take the Producer's view into account, where possible, provided, that it is understood that the Distributor shall have the right to make the final decision.

"**Mobile Device**" means any mobile wireless device (whether now known or hereafter developed), including, without limitation, a personal digital assistant (PDA) or mobile phone, which is capable of receiving and sending voice and/or data and/or video communications by means of Mobile Wireless Technology and which is designed or adapted to be capable of being used while the user is in motion but excluding portable television sets.

"Mobile Wireless Technology" means any mobile wireless technology, which is or may be commercially deployed during the Term with radio frequency spectrum in any band, to enable or facilitate transmission of textual material, data, voice, video or multimedia services to Mobile Devices and which includes (without limitation) wireless technology employed in General Packet Radio Services (GPRS), the Global System for Mobile Communications (GSM), Enhanced Data GSM Environment (EDGE), Code Division Multiple Access (CDMA), High-Speed Circuit Switched Data (HSCSD), Personal Communications Networks (PCN), Wireless Application Protocol (WAP) and the Universal Mobile Telecommunications System (UMTS) and their related or derivative systems and services or any combination of them but excluding the following wireless radio communications systems, namely 802.11, Wi-Fi, Bluetooth, Wireless LAN technologies, HiperLAN, Local Multipoint Distribution System (LMDS), Multichannel Multipoint Distribution System (MMDS) and any related, similar or derivative wireless radio communications systems or any combination of them.

"Motion Film or Television Series" means an audiovisual work consisting of a series of related images that, when shown in succession, impart an impression of motion, with accompanying sounds, if any.

"Motion Film or Television Series Copy" means the embodiment of a Motion Film or Television Series in any physical form, including without limitation film, tape, cassette, or disc. Where a specific medium is limited to exploitation by a specific physical form, then Motion Film or Television Series Copy is limited to such physical form.

"Non-Residential Pay-Per-View" means the broadcast of a Motion Film or Television Series Copy by means of an encoded signal (whether analog, digital or otherwise) including DBS and DVB for reception on television transmission receivers in hotels, motels or similar temporary living places where a charge is made to the viewer for the right to use a decoding device to view the broadcast of the Motion Film or Television Series (or a specific group of programs) at a time designated by the broadcaster for each viewing.

"Non-Theatrical" means the exploitation of a Motion Film or Television Series Copy for direct exhibition before an audience by and at the facilities of either institutions or organizations not primarily engaged in the business of exhibiting Motion Films or Television Series, such as educational organizations, churches, restaurants, bars, clubs, trains, libraries, Red Cross facilities, oil rigs, and oil fields, or by and at the facilities of governmental bodies such as embassies, military bases, military vessels and other governmental bodies flying the flag of the licensed territory. By way of clarification, Non-Theatrical does not include exploitation of the Film or Television Series by Theatrical, Public Video, Commercial Video, Airlines, Ship, or Hotel exploitation.

"On-Demand/Demand View" means the making available of a Motion Picture or Television Series Copy (whether analog or digital) by means of an encoded signal enabling the viewer/user to demand the signal(s)—irrespective of the technology/system used to meet such demand, the means by which signals are carried and whether a charge is made to the viewer/user or not—at a time and place selected by the viewer/user.

"Party" means either the Producer or the Distributor.

"Pay-TV" means all forms of Terrestrial Pay-TV, Cable Pay-TV, and Satellite Pay-TV exploitation of a Motion Film or Television Series. Pay-TV does not include any form of "pay-per-view" telecast or other exhibition not specified herein.

"Pay-Per-View" or "PPV" means Non-Residential Pay-Per-View or Residential Pay-Per-View exploitation of a Motion Film or Television Series. Pay-Per-View does not include any form of Pay-TV or Free TV. It means the transmission of an encrypted television signal by means of a point-to-multipoint distribution system, whereby (i) the transmission of the Program originates from a transmission source outside of the user's dwelling unit; (ii) the scheduling of the exhibition of the Program is predetermined, in whole or in part, by the distribution service; and (iii) the viewer is required to pay or is assessed a separate per-program, per-exhibition fee (including pay-per-day and so-called near video on demand), as opposed to payment being on a pre-packaged, subscription basis.

"Person" means any natural or legal entity.

"Principal Photography" means the actual photographing of a Motion Film or Television Series, excluding second-unit photography or special photography, requiring the participation of the director and the on-camera participation of a featured member of the principal cast.

"Producer" means the party to this Agreement that owns or otherwise has the full and unlimited right to license the Granted Rights to the Distributor and includes the Producer's agents, administrators, successors, and assigns; it may also be referred to as the "Licensor."

"Program" means the film, television, video and/or multi-media program or programs or show(s) licensed by the Producer to the Distributor hereunder.

"Public Video" means the exploitation of a Motion Film or Television Series Copy embodied in a Videogram only for direct exhibition before an audience in a "mini-Theatre," an "MTV Theatre" or like establishment that charges an admission to use the viewing facility or to view the Videogram and that is not licensed as a traditional motion picture theatre in the place where the viewing occurs.

"Publishing Rights" means exploitation of hardcover or softcover printed publications of a novelization of the Program or artwork, logos, or photographic stills created for use in the Program that is included in such novelization.

"Residential Pay-Per-View" means the broadcast of a Motion Film or Television Series Copy transmission by means of an encoded signal (whether analog, digital or otherwise) including DBS and DVB for the reception on television receivers in homes or similar living places where a charge is made to the viewer for the right to use a decoding device to view the broadcast of the Motion Film or Television Series (or a specific group of programs) at a time designated by the broadcaster for each viewing.

"Rights" means rights, licenses, and privileges under copyright, trademark, neighboring rights, or other intellectual property rights with regard to any type of exploitation of a Motion Film or Television Series or its Underlying Material.

"Royalty Income" All amounts collected by any collecting society, authors' rights organization, performing rights society or government agency arising from compulsory licenses, cable retransmission income, music performance royalties, tax rebates, exhibition surcharges, levies on blank Videograms or hardware, rental or lending royalties.

"Run" means one (1) telecast of the Program during a twenty-four (24) hour period over the non-overlapping telecast facilities of an authorized telecaster such that the Program is only capable of reception on television receivers within the reception zone of such telecaster once during such period. A simultaneous telecast over several interconnected local stations (i.e., on a network) constitutes one (1) telecast; a telecast over non-interconnected local stations whose signal reception areas do not overlap constitutes a telecast in each station's local broadcast area.

"Satellite Free TV" means only the uplink transmission (whether analog, digital or otherwise) of a Motion Film or Television Series Copy to a satellite and its downlink transmission to a terrestrial satellite reception dish for the purpose of viewing the Motion Film or Television Series on a television receiver in private living accommodations which is located in the immediate vicinity of the reception dish without a charge being made to the viewer for the privilege of viewing the Film or Television Series. For the purposes of this definition, neither governmental television receiver assessments or taxes (but not a charge for Pay-Per-View or Pay-TV) will be deemed a charge to the viewer.

"Ship" means any vessel or shipping line facilitating or permitting the exploitation of a Motion Film or Television Series Copy for direct exhibition at sea or on ocean-going vessels, which are operated by a shipping line flying the flag of any country in the licensed territory for which Ship exploitation is granted, and including shipping lines and/or sea or ocean-going vessels which are mainly serviced in but do not fly the flag of a country in the licensed territory.

"Stream" or **"Streaming"** means transmission of a digital copy of the Program, via software which enables the continuous delivery of audio and/or audio-visual transmission to a Licensed Device which delivery is configured to prevent Downloading or other copying upon reception so that the recipient is unable to retain any copy, including a cached copy, of any such transmission within the recipient's possession beyond the real-time presentation of the transmission to the recipient.

"Subscription Video On Demand" or **"SVOD"** means the transmission of the Program chosen by a user to a television or Licensed Device where: (i) the commencement time for the transmission of the Program is at the user's sole discretion and is not predetermined or scheduled by the Licensed Service; (ii) the transmission of the Program originates from a source outside of the user's residence or Licensed Device, as applicable; (iii) the transmission of the Program is commercial-free, linear and uninterrupted; (iv) the user may view such program an unlimited number of times during the calendar month for which the user has paid.

"Satellite Pay TV" means the uplink transmission of a Motion Film or Television Series Copy by means of an encoded signal (whether analog, digital or otherwise) to a satellite and its downlink transmission to a terrestrial satellite reception dish and a decoding device for the purpose of viewing the Film or Television Series on a television receiver in private or temporary living accommodations which are located in the immediate vicinity of the reception dish and decoding device where a charge is made: (i) to the viewer in private living accommodations for the right to use the decoding device for viewing any special channel which transmits the Motion Picture along with other programming; or (ii) to the operator of a hotel or motel (or similar temporary living place), apartment complex, co-operative, condominium project or similar place located at a distance from the place where such broadcast signal originated for the right use the decoding device to receive and retransmit the programming on such a channel throughout such places.

"Television Rights" means together with Free TV Rights and Pay-TV Rights.

"Term" means the period of time during which a Distributor is acquiring the Granted Rights pursuant to this Agreement.

"Terrestrial Free TV" means only standard over-the-air broadcast (whether analog, digital or otherwise), by means of Hertzian waves, of a Motion Film or Television Series Copy which is intended for reception on a television receiver in private living accommodations without charge being made to the viewer for the privilege of viewing the Motion Film or Television Series. For the purposes of this definition, neither governmental television receiver assessments or taxes (but not a charge for Pay-Per-View or Pay-TV) will be deemed a charge to the viewer. Terrestrial Free TV does not include any form of Free TV, PPV, VOD or SVOD.

"Terrestrial Pay-TV" means only standard over-the-air broadcast of a Motion Film or Television Series Copy, by means of encoded Hertzian waves (whether analog, digital or otherwise), for reception on a television receiver in private or temporary living accommodations by means of a decoding device where a charge is made: (i) to the viewer in private living accommodations for the right to use the decoding device for viewing any special channel that transmits the Motion Picture along with other programming; or (ii) to the operator of a hotel or motel (or similar temporary living place), apartment complex, co-operative, condominium project or similar place located at a distance from the place where such a broadcast signal originated for the right to use the decoding device to receive and retransmit the programming on such a channel throughout such places. Terrestrial Pay-TV does not include any form of Free TV, PPV, VOD or SVOD.

"Territory" means the geographic area and/or program markets in which the Distributor is licensed to sell, license, distribute, sub-distribute, broadcast, transmit and otherwise commercially exploit the Program pursuant to this Agreement.

"Theatrical" means the exploitation of the Motion Film or Television Series in whatever format including, but not limited to, 70mm, 35mm, 16mm or by means of digital transfer to the viewing place only for direct exhibition in conventional or drive-in theatres, licensed as such in the place where the exhibition occurs, that are open to the general public on a regularly scheduled basis and that charge an admission fee to view the Motion Film or Television Series.

"Underlying Material" means the literary and other material from which a Motion Film or Television Series is derived, or on which it is based, including all versions of the screenplay, all notes, memos, direction, comments, ideas, stage business and other material incorporated in any version of the Motion Film or Television Series, and, to the extent necessary, for which rights and licenses have been duly obtained, and all existing novels, stories, plays, songs, events, characters, ideas or other works from which any version of the Motion Film or Television Series is derived or on which it is based.

"Version" means an adaptation of a Motion Film or Television Series that is not accomplished by merely mechanical reproduction or use of minimal originality but that instead used original artistic or intellectual expression to create a new Work in its own right which contains materials or expressions of authorship not found in the original Motion Film or Television Series.

"Video" means the Home Video and/or Commercial Video exploitation of a Motion Film or Television Series.

"Videocassette" means a VHS or Beta cassette or comparable storage device in any authorized format designed to be used in conjunction with a reproduction apparatus that causes a Motion Film or Television Series to be visible on the screen of a television receiver for viewing in a substantially linear manner. A Videocassette does not include any type of Videodisc, other Videogram devices, or Compact Disc.

"Videodisc" means a laser or capacitance disc or comparable optical or mechanical storage device designed to be used with a reproduction apparatus that causes a Motion Film or Television Series to be visible on the screen of a television receiver for viewing in a substantially linear manner. A Videodisc does not include any type of Videocassette, other Videogram devices, or Compact Disc.

"Videogram" means any type of Videocassette, Videodisc, CD-ROM, CD-Recordable, DVD, magnet bands, discs, chips, memory sticks, and other devices that are capable of supporting a video signal.

"VOD" means a device permitting a user, on an individual basis, to view a Program on a television or Licensed Device where: (i) the commencement time for the transmission of the Program is at the user's sole discretion, and is not predetermined or scheduled by the Licensed Service; (ii) the transmission of the Program originates from a source other than a user's residence or a user's Licensed Device, as applicable; (iii) the transmission of the Program is commercial-free, linear and uninterrupted; and (iv) the user is assessed a per-transmission or per-Program fee.

"VOD Rights" means the right to distribute the Program via VOD.

"Web TV" means the broadcast of a Motion Film or Television Series Copy via DVB including, but not limited to, any form of broadcasting and/or streaming via all online packet-switching communication systems whether publicly available or not and includes any DVB like exploitation via the world wide web (www).

"**Work**" means an original expression of authorship in the literary, scientific, or artistic domain, whatever may be the mode or form of its expression.

2. PARTICULARS

PROGRAM # 1:
DURATION: __x__ episodes _x_ minutes each
PRODUCTION YEAR:
TERRITORY: Exclusivity in the entire world with the exception of _____.
ORIGINAL VERSION: English
VERSIONS AVAILABLE:
SUBTITLE: TBA
CRTC/CAVCO #:
TERM: xx years from delivery of all the materials from the Producer and acceptance from the Distributor, to be automatically renewed annually for a further xx years unless terminated by written notice of at least xx calendar months by either Party to the other, to expire on the last day of the initial period or on any anniversary thereof. After the expiration of the last renewal, the Distributor shall have the first negotiation and last refusal to continue the distribution of the Program under the same terms and conditions of the present document.
RIGHTS: All rights. As described in article 3.3.
NUMBER OF TRANSMISSIONS, BROADCASTS, CABLECASTS FOR PROGRAM # 1: Unlimited

PROGRAM # 2:
DURATION: __x__ episodes _x_ minutes each
PRODUCTION YEAR:
TERRITORY: Exclusivity in the entire world with the exception of _____.
ORIGINAL VERSION: English
VERSIONS AVAILABLE:
SUBTITLE: TBA
CRTC/CAVCO #:
TERM: xx years from delivery of all the materials from the Producer and acceptance from the Distributor, to be automatically renewed annually for a further xx years unless terminated by written notice of at least xx calendar months from by either Party to the other, to expire on the last day of the initial period or on any anniversary thereof. After the expiration of the last renewal, the Distributor shall have the first negotiation and last refusal to continue the distribution of the Program under the same terms and conditions of the present document.
RIGHTS: All rights. As described in article 3.3.
NUMBER OF TRANSMISSIONS, BROADCASTS, CABLECASTS FOR PROGRAM # 1: Unlimited

CROSS-COLLATERALIZATION: The Parties agree that a Cross-Collateralization must be part of this Agreement between the Distributor and the Producer to pool their guarantees in handling the distribution.

3. DISTRIBUTOR'S RIGHTS

3.1 The Distributor has the right to pre-sell the show(s) from the delivery of the scripts prior to the start of the term. The Distributor reserves the right to terminate the agreement subject to the approval of the script. If the show(s) have been already produced and finished at the time of the signature of this agreement, the Distributor has the right to sell the show(s) subject to the approval of the material. The Distributor reserves the right to terminate the agreement subject to the approval of the material delivered by the Producer.

3.2 The Distributor shall have first negotiation and last refusal for the distribution and/or co-production on subsequent show(s), movies, any format containing the characters in the Program, or any show(s) based substantially on the Program, under the same terms and conditions of the present document.

3.3 The Producer grants to the Distributor the exclusive right to distribute and to appoint sub-agents and sub-distributors to distribute the Program in all languages throughout the Territory during the Term to all media and in all formats and technical configurations whether now or hereafter known, including but not limited to Cinematic, Television Rights, Theatrical, Non-Theatrical, Public Video, Ancillary Video, Home Video, Commercial Video, Home Video Rental, Home Video Sell Through, High definition, Digital Television (DTV), MMS, SMS or any phone system, free television, cable television, Pay-TV: Terrestrial Pay-TV, Cable Pay-TV, Satellite Pay-TV, WEB TV, PPV/Pay-Per-View: Non-Residential Pay-Per-View, Residential Pay-Per-View, subscription television, over-the-air pay television, Free TV: Terrestrial Free TV, Cable Free TV, Satellite Free TV, closed circuit television, master antenna television, direct broadcast satellite (DBS) television, DVB (Digital Video Broadcast), DVD-ROM, DVD-RAM, Consumer acquisition (HDV) and optical disc systems (HDDVD and Blu-ray), video-on-demand, armed forces, in-flight use on Airlines, use on Ships, video cassettes and video discs for home use, non-theatrical uses (including but not limited to educational institutions, clubs, hospitals, embassies and means of transport), mobile devices, broadband, mobile wireless technology, Publishing Rights, IPTV, Stream or Streaming, Subscription Video On Demand or SVOD, Video On Demand or VOD, all music rights, internet and e-commerce rights, Interactive Multimedia, Interactive Networked Multimedia, Interactive Multimedia Work, Compact Disc Interactive, Compact Disc, Laser Disc, Videocassette, Videogram, Videodisc, merchandising (manufacture, distribution, sale and advertising in the Territory of merchandise articles of every type and description including, but not limited to, games and computer games) and publishing rights (including publication in electronic or other interactive form), or in translation, books and other publications based on or utilizing the copyright or trademarks.

3.4 The Distributor may sub-license any rights licensed by the Producer hereunder for a period that survives the Term.

3.5 The Producer shall be bound by any and all agreements with third parties negotiated and entered into by the Distributor with respect to the Program.

3.6 The Distributor shall have all normal and customary rights of distributors for the Program in the Territory, including, without limitation, the unqualified control of the distribution, exploitation and other disposition of the Program directly or by any subsidiary, affiliate, sub-distributor, or any other party, in accordance with such terms and conditions, including, but not limited to, price and change of title, as the Distributor in its sole discretion may determine.

3.7 The Distributor shall have the right to sell any of the Program format(s) or derivative works to a third party. In this event, the Distributor fees will be the same as those established in paragraph 4.1 of this Agreement: (35%) from all its receipts arising from the sales of the format of the Program for any and all audiovisual media from the gross revenues.

4. DISTRIBUTION FEES

4.1 The Distributor shall be entitled to deduct and retain 35% from all its receipts arising from its distribution of the Program(s) for all audiovisual media from the gross revenues. Gross distribution fees are computed prior to the deduction of withholding tax (if any) at the source. Gross revenues received by the Distributor under this paragraph will be allocated and paid as follows:

(a) first, the fees referred to in the first sentence of this paragraph 4.1 (distribution fees) shall be deducted;
(b) then dubbing/mix and/or subtitling costs of the version in the language of the buying territory, and distribution expenses; For clarification: distribution expenses are screening materials, promotional material and couriers, marketing expenses, market attendance, flyers, brochures, advertising, printed materials, posters, images, web digitization, reasonable market expenses, transmission materials for contracted sales (DigiBetas/hard drive/Transparencies/Scripts/Couriers for delivery, etc.) recoupable from the Producer's share. In the event, extra costs or expenses are incurred, they will be recoupable from the Producer's share.
(c) next, the expenses referred to in paragraphs 4.6, 4.7 and 4.8 (but without any duplication of deductions made under paragraphs 4.1(a) and (b)) will be deducted;

(d) the balance will be paid to the Producer (after an approved invoice is provided to the Distributor and upon the buyer's acceptance of the materials and full and complete payment is received by the Distributor).

4.2 All distribution fees are based on gross license fees and are computed prior to the deduction of withholding tax (if any) at the source.

4.3 In the event of a theatrical sale, the Producer shall provide the Distributor, free of charge, with the necessary copies of the Program for the fulfillment of the contracted distribution agreement.

4.4 The Producer grants and licenses to the Distributor a beneficial interest in and the exclusive right to collect, throughout the Territory during the Term, all royalties, fees and other revenues which the Producer, or the registered copyright owner, is otherwise entitled to collect by reason of any statute, governmental regulation, operation of law or in any other manner, for, based upon or in connection with, in whole or in part, or directly or indirectly, any use of the Program pursuant to any exercise of the Rights granted hereunder, including the recording and/or retransmission of the signal embodying the program ("Copyright Revenues"). All Copyright Revenues derived by the Distributor shall be included in the Gross Receipts, including but not limited to: music, director, scripts, treatment, author's rights and all and any rights, and will be collected through the Distributor who will keep the same fee of 35%. It is also agreed that in the event that any pre-sale or final sale is done and the buyer cancels the agreement due to failure of delivery by the Producer or because the Producer is late on its production schedule as agreed upon in this Agreement, then the Distributor shall be entitled to its distribution fees (35% of the gross) and costs as if the sale was fully executed and the Distributor will have the right to proceed against any claims and pursue its remedies.

4.5 In the event that the Producer fails to perform, and the Distributor has to advance any monies and/or services for operational purposes, the Distributor will be entitled to the recoupment of the advanced monies that will be deducted from gross sales, plus standard bank interest.

4.6 The Distributor is entitled to deduct and retain 35% from all its receipts arising from its distribution of the Program of gross revenue from the monies due to the Producer or claim from the Producer upon termination, to cover any and all un-recouped allowable expenses and all/any advanced monies and/or services due to failure to perform by the Producer for operational cost purposes. However, this 35% shall not include the following, which are in addition to those items mentioned in paragraph 4.1(b):

- for all merchandising and publishing rights.
- duplication of masters for sale.

- duplication and conversion of masters and creation of M&E tracks (if not supplied by the Producer)
- collection of monies from the Distributors and sub-distributors (including all reasonable legal fees).

4.7 In the event that the Distributor appoints sub-agents and sub-distributors when/whereas per the Distributor's judgment they are required for the distribution of the Program any commissions and fees payable to such sub-agents and sub-distributors shall, except where otherwise agreed with the Producer, be contained within the Distribution Fees payable to and costs recoupable by the Distributor hereunder.

4.8 As a condition precedent to the payment of any monies which may become due and payable under this Agreement, the Producer agrees that it shall provide to the Distributor the complete chain-of-title documentation relating to the Producer. The Producer shall deliver the Program no later than a date to be advised and accepted by the Distributor (the "Delivery Date"). "Complete Delivery" shall mean complete and technically acceptable delivery of the Program by the Producer to the Distributor, and the acceptance thereof, in writing, by the Distributor. Complete Delivery is a condition precedent to all of the Distributor's obligations hereunder. In the event that the Distributor elects in its sole discretion to create any delivery element that the Producer is unable to supply, the Distributor shall have the right to recoup the cost of such an element plus the "Servicing Fee" from the Gross Receipts outside of any cap, if any, on Expenses. In the event that the Distributor elects in its sole discretion to create any delivery elements which the Producer is unable to supply, the Distributor shall have the right to recoup the cost of such elements plus a 20% "Servicing Fee" from the Gross Receipts outside of any cap on Expenses and bank interest. In the event that the Producer's share of the Gross Receipts becomes payable prior to Complete Delivery, the Distributor has the right to withhold a reasonable estimation of the cost of completing any missing delivery element from any payment due to the Producer until such missing element(s) are delivered.

4.9 The Producer further agrees without further consideration, in future, to do such further acts and execute and deliver to the Distributor such further assignments, waivers, applications, documents or assurances as the Distributor, acting reasonably, may request, to vest, effect, perfect, register, record, verify, evidence or enforce its rights and interests, including copyright, in the above-mentioned Program, or derivative works.

5. **TRANSMISSION MATERIALS**

5.1 The Producer will, at its expense, lodge and insure an HD Master tape as well as Digital Pal and NTSC master videotapes of (each of) the Program together with a separate M&E track with the Distributor. The Producer will authorize the Distributor to fulfill the Distributor's orders for transmission materials and other copies duplicated from the master as the Distributor may reasonably require the cost of, which insofar as the same, is not paid for or reimbursed by the Distributor of the Program, shall be recouped from net income due to the Producer in the event that the Producer cannot fulfill its duty of sending the transmission material in a time-efficient manner, and based only on the Distributor's final decision.

5.2 The Producer shall deliver the Program, in a technical quality equivalent to that of a first-class television program broadcast or cinema-standard in Canada.

5.3 The Distributor shall have the right to add or include a prominent credit for itself as the Distributor of the Program, including its own name and/or logo and/or trademark, in and on all publicity material, printed matter, merchandising and on all copies of the Program sold, licensed or otherwise distributed. For programs not yet edited, such credit will be added during the editing process and provided to the Producer by the Distributor on videotape; such credits and logos cannot be deleted or modified under any circumstances and must be included in any copy of the Program to be distributed or not by the Distributor even if this Agreement is canceled. The Producer will be solely responsible for any and all expenses related to these actions.

6. **CONFIDENTIALITY AND CIRCUMVENTION**

6.1 The Producer recognizes that, in connection with the performance of this Agreement, the Distributor may disclose or the Producer might have access to, technical information, including without limitation, information about the Distributor and or the property and strategies, promotions, customers, the terms of this Agreement and other similar contracts, and related non-technical business information which the Distributor considers to be confidential ("Confidential Information"). The Producer agrees to maintain the confidential status of such Confidential Information and not to use any such Confidential Information for any purpose other than the purpose for which it was originally disclosed to the Producer and not to disclose any of such Confidential Information to any third party.

6.2 The Producer shall cause its directors, officers and employees to keep confidential the names and contact information of the banks, trusts, lenders or borrowers, lending institutions, corporations, buyers, sellers, groups and individuals introduced by the Distributor or their associates and to use such information only for the purpose of carrying out the Producer's obligations under this Agreement. Such information is considered the property of the Distributor and shall remain so for the term of this Agreement.

6.3 The Producer shall not circumvent, bypass, or obviate the Distributor, directly or indirectly, to avoid payment of fees or commissions to which the Distributor is entitled under the terms of this Agreement, in such transactions with any Person revealed by either Party to the other.

6.4 In the event of circumvention, either directly or indirectly, the Distributor shall be entitled to a legal monetary penalty equal to the maximum service fee/commission standard in the industry, which would be the result of such a transaction. This payment to be increased to include all reasonable legal expenses incurred in the recovery of this monetary penalty.

7. REPRESENTATIONS AND WARRANTIES

7.1 The Producer undertakes with and represents and warrants to the Distributor as follows:

(i) The Producer is the owner of or controls all the rights in the Program which are granted to the Distributor hereunder, and that the Producer will have secured the consents in writing of all artists and/or other persons whose performances or the products of whose services are reproduced in the Program in accordance with the License in the Particulars (subject to the restrictions (if any) in the Particulars) and for the unrestricted use and publication by the Distributor of all promotional artwork supplied by the Producer and of the legal and professional names, photographs, likenesses, and biographies of the artists, characters, and other persons whose performances or the product of whose services are reproduced in the Program.

There are no rights, licenses or grants of any nature in favour of anyone which would impair, diminish or infringe upon the Granted Rights; and that the Producer has not done and will not do anything, whether by act, omission, agreement or any other means, to impair or interfere with the full enjoyment by the Distributor of the Granted Rights;

(ii) That the Distributor shall be under no liability whatsoever to any of the said artist's characters and other persons or to any third party arising out of the exercise by it or any third party authorized by it of the rights hereby granted in accordance with the terms of this Agreement.

(iii) To the extent which the Program incorporates library or third party materials of any nature the Producer has obtained license from the copyright owners thereof in order to enable the Program to be exploited and distributed during the Term to all broadcast, satellite, and cable television markets and to all home video and non-theatrical and educational markets in all countries within the Territory or to the extent that such licenses shall not have been obtained the Producer shall advise the Distributor and at the Distributor's request and the Producer's expense, obtain the same and pay all necessary license fees to the copyright owners.

(iv) The Producer has paid or will pay all sums due to any third party who is or may be entitled to any payment in respect of services or facilities rendered or goods supplied or rights granted in respect of the Program.

(v) The performing rights in any musical work reproduced by the Program are controlled by the Performing Right Society or an affiliated collecting society or are in the public domain.

(vi) There are no claims, liens or encumbrances to the best of the Producer's knowledge and belief, of any nature affecting the Program or any part or parts thereof and there is no litigation pending or threatened with respect to the Program or any element or any right therein which would or might affect any of the rights granted to the Distributor hereunder.

(vii) Neither the Program nor any portion thereof is in any way defamatory to any copyright, license, right to privacy, right of publicity or any other right of any person, organization, firm or company or government;

(viii) The Producer will keep the Distributor fully indemnified from, and against all liabilities, claims, actions, proceedings, damages, costs, and loss (including but not limited to reasonable legal fees) suffered or incurred by the Distributor or awarded against the Distributor as a consequence of or arising from:

> (a) any breach or non-performance of any of the covenants, representations and/or warranties set out in this Agreement unless such breach or non-performance results from an act or omission of the Distributor; and
>
> (b) any use by the Distributor and/or by any third party authorized or permitted by the Distributor of the Program in any manner authorized under this Agreement provided that any such claims are finally adjudicated or are settled with the prior written consent of the Producer.

(ix) The Program is not subject to the jurisdiction of any union, guild or collective bargaining association and the Producer additionally grants to the Distributor the right to change the title of the Program and to cut, edit, dub, subtitle and alter the Program or any parts thereof, and to authorize others to do so, as the Distributor may deem necessary for the effective marketing, distribution, and exploitation of the Program.

7.2 The Distributor undertakes with and represents and warrants to the Producer as follows:

(i) To use all reasonable endeavours and good business judgment to market, distribute, and exploit the Program to all viable markets throughout the Territory.

(ii) To include the Program in the Distributor's catalogue of programs available for exploitation within the Territory.

(iii) To offer the Program for sale and distribution to third parties at all national and international markets, trade fairs, and festivals attended by the Distributor.

(iv) The Distributor will use its best endeavours (which shall not, however, unless specifically agreed with the Producer in writing, oblige the Distributor to institute legal proceedings) (a) to prevent any infringement by any person, firm, or corporation to whom or to which the Distributor has sold or distributed the Program or by any customer of any such person, firm, or corporation of the copyright in (any of) the Program which may come to its notice and/or (b) to recover proper damages or compensation arising from any such infringement, provided that any damages or compensation recovered hereunder shall, after deduction of any irrecoverable costs, be divided in accordance with the commission agreed upon between the Distributor and the Producer and the Producer's share thereof shall be paid by the Distributor within thirty-five (35) days of the end of the quarterly period in which the Distributor receives the same.

8. **STATEMENTS**

8.1   The Distributor shall provide to the Producer (as well during as after the Term for so long as the Distributor continues to receive gross license fees or receipts from sub-distributors as referred to below) detailed statements showing:

i) The gross license fees received by the Distributor.

ii) Any extra commission payable to a sub-agent by the Distributor from the gross license fees where permitted hereunder, provided that any such extra commission shall be paid only after receipts have been received in full by the Distributor.

iii) Any other permitted costs recoupable from sums due to the Producer.

iv) Withhold tax if any deducted at the source from the gross license fees under paragraph (i) above or actual receipts under paragraph (ii) above.

8.2 The Distributor shall pay to the Producer with each statement referred to in paragraph 8.1 the balance if any is remaining in U.S. dollars (unless otherwise agreed with the Producer in advance) payable in accordance with section 4.1.

8.3 The Distributor will use its best endeavours (which shall not, however, unless specifically agreed with the Producer in any particular case, oblige the Distributor to institute legal proceedings for recovery of unpaid monies) to collect from its licensees and sub-distributors and others, all license fees and other payments contractually due to it from its distribution hereunder of the Program.

9. BOOKS OF ACCOUNTS

9.1 The Distributor shall keep full accurate and up-to-date records of all its transactions and books of accounts relating to the subject matter of this Agreement. The Producer shall have the right, at the Producer's own expense, to inspect, examine, copy and take extracts from the licenses and other agreements and records of the Distributor insofar as such licenses and other agreements and records pertain to the Program but not further or otherwise. Such inspection shall be made after 31 days written notice and during normal business hours. The right to inspect shall not extend beyond 1 month from the expiry of the Term or the expiry of any agreement entered into by the Distributor in respect to the Program which survives the Term, whichever is the later.

9.2 In the event that exchange control or other currency restrictions shall prohibit or restrict the remittance to the Distributor in Canada of any monies which, if so remitted and after deduction of sums due to the Distributor hereunder, would result in monies payable to the Producer hereunder, the Distributor shall promptly inform the Producer by notice in writing and if requested by the Producer and if the Distributor is able to do so, shall either deposit such monies into a bank account nominated by the Producer in the country prohibiting or restricting such remittance in the name of and for the sole benefit of the Producer or pay such monies to a third party designated by the Producer in such a country.

9.3 The Distributor shall, in respect to all tax which it is obliged by law to be withheld at the source whether directly or indirectly from any payments to the Producer under this Agreement, supply to the Producer a withholding tax certificate where available or such other evidence of such withholding as the Producer may reasonably require.

10. TERMINATION

10.1 In the event that during the Term:

(i) Any sums due from the Distributor to the Producer (for which the Producer shall furnish the Distributor with all the details needed to fulfill the Distributor's duties, including invoice, bank details, etc.) under this Agreement will be overdue by forty-five (45) days or more following the buyer's written approval of materials and once payment is fully received in the Distributor's bank account, and the Distributor has not made payment thereof in full within forty-five (45) days of the Distributor's receipt from the Producer of written notice of such breach; or

(ii) The Distributor shall commit any material breach of the terms of this Agreement which is not capable of remedy or which is capable of remedy but is not remedied within forty-five (45) business days of the Distributor's receipt from the Producer of written notice of such breach; or

(iii) The Distributor shall cease to carry out business in the Territory as a program distributor; or

(iv) The Distributor shall make any assignment for the benefit of or make any composition with creditors or if any action or proceeding under bankruptcy or insolvency law is taken against the Distributor including, without limitation, the appointment of a receiver liquidator or trustee in bankruptcy or if the Distributor shall effect a voluntary or compulsory liquidation of assets (other than for purposes of amalgamation or reconstruction; then the Producer shall be entitled to terminate this Agreement with immediate effect by giving notice in writing to the Distributor, provided that such termination shall not affect or prejudice the rights and remedies of the Parties arising prior to the date of such termination. Such termination may relate to this Agreement as a whole or only to the country or countries of the Territory in respect to which the breach complained of occurs as the Producer may elect at its own discretion.

10.2 In the event that this distribution agreement expires or is terminated for any reason other than termination by the Producer for a reason set out in paragraph 10.1, the Distributor shall have twelve months to finalize all pending deals. If a buyer requires extra time to acquire the Program, the Distributor will inform the Producer who will grant up to another four months for this purpose. If the Producer approaches any of the Distributors' contacts to finalize a negotiation already started by the Distributor, the Distributor shall be entitled to receive its 35% commission fee as set out in paragraph 4.1.

10.3 At the expiry or earlier lawful termination of the Term (howsoever arising):

(i) The Distributor's rights hereunder in respect to the Program and all copies and other derivatives and materials relating thereto whether or not supplied or created hereunder shall forthwith cease (except insofar as the same relate to any agreement entered into by the Distributor in respect to the Program which survives such expiry or earlier lawful termination);

(ii) The Distributor shall promptly send such copies and other derivatives and materials (the cost of which shall be paid by the Producer) to the Producer or to such a third party as the Producer shall designate (where appropriate in the same condition as the same was delivered to the Distributor (only reasonable wear and tear accepted)) or promptly destroy or erase the same (if so requested by the Producer) and furnish to the Producer in respect thereof a certificate of destruction or erasure in a form acceptable to the Producer.

10.4 Notwithstanding anything to the contrary contained in this Agreement, if either Party shall be delayed in or prevented from performing any of its obligations under this Agreement for any reason beyond such party's control (save in the case of a failure by the Distributor to make any payment due to the Producer by reason of a lack of funds) then such non-performance shall be deemed not to constitute a breach of this Agreement. If this Agreement cannot be enforced or performed according to its terms for a period in excess of six (6) months, it shall be deemed to have been terminated at the end of such a six (6) month period, provided that if any such reason applies in respect to only one or more countries of the Territory, such termination shall apply to such a country or countries only.

10.5 Save where provision is made to the contrary, hereunder, any notice under the provisions hereof shall be in writing and shall be sufficiently served if sent by pre-paid postage or facsimile or similar system which prints or reproduces the notice at the receiving end upon dispatch if sent to the address or the facsimile number of the party to be served last known to the party serving such a notice and shall be deemed to have been received (if sent by pre-paid postage) seven (7) days following the date of posting thereof or (if sent by facsimile or similar system as aforesaid) upon dispatch and shall be deemed to have been received simultaneously except that a notice that is given or served on a Saturday or Sunday or public holiday shall not be deemed given until the commencement of normal business hours on the next weekday.

10.6 This Agreement shall not be assignable by the Producer or the Distributor in whole or in part without the written consent of the other party which may be granted or withheld at its discretion, provided however that the Distributor may enter into sub-agency, sub-distribution and sub-license agreements as contemplated in this Agreement.

11. **RIGHTS OF DISTRIBUTOR**

The Distributor shall be entitled throughout the Territory during the Term to authorize others at no cost to the Producer:

11.1   To use the present title(s) or any translation(s) thereof of the Program in connection with the distribution, exhibition, exploitation, advertising and any other uses thereof to change said title(s) and to use any other title(s) in any language to designate the Program, but no warranty of the Producer shall be applicable to (any of) the changed title(s).

11.2   To arrange or commission the subtitling and dubbing of the Program in any language spoken in the Territory and make subtitled and dubbed language versions of the Program for use in the Territory.

11.3   To edit, re-cut, re-edit or delete any pictures and/or sound material in the Program and any prints, cassettes and/or other derivatives of the Program in such a manner and to such extent in order to enable the Program to be distributed and exhibited in any country within the Territory.

12. DELIVERABLES

12.1 The Producer will start sending materials as they become available and no later than a week from the Delivery Date (such a date to be confirmed in writing by the Producer and the Distributor) to the Distributor. When further materials not included in the following list are required by the Distributor, the Producer shall provide the Distributor with the required materials no later than a week from the Distributor's request at the Producer's expense:

For TV Release:

1.1 Two hard drives one with a PAL Digital version and one an NTSC Digital version of the Program along with a QC report for the hard drive, with separate tracks for a soundtrack (English version. Ratio HDTV 16:9). At the end of the show, the textless version must include:

- at least 1 minute of colour bars and tone at the head
- a head slate and an exterior label are identifying the production company, the name of the production, the track assignments, the length, the date of creation, and any other relevant information relating to the identification of the finished product.

Track Assignments: Stereo Left and Right (Full Mix) on Channels 1 & 2 and Stereo Music and Effects (M&E) on Channels 3 & 4.

This must be a full-frame (i.e., Non-letterboxed) new, first-generation version.
i.   Trailer with the same technical specifications as the hard drives.

ii. A music cue sheet indicating: title, duration, composer, lyricist, publisher, and performing arts society for each musical work contained in the show.(See appendix 4)
iii. Full style guide or manual of style
iv. Free access to copies of the released material in all languages, if any.
v. One complete set of copies of all clearances and title documents for the Program. At distributor request.
vi. Quality Control Certificate. At the distributor's request.
vii. A letter guaranteeing permission to distribute.
viii. One printed copy music cue sheet and one electronic format.
ix. Biographies of all creative personnel (actors, writers, directors, and Producers).
x. All available press cuttings.
xi. Sample publicity/advertising/merchandising material as reasonably requested by the Distributor.
xii. Time-coded post-production script indicating the full running length in any/all available language(s).
xiii. Synopsis of the Program.
xiv. Twenty colour transparencies and Twenty black and white digital images with numbered captions.
xv. One copy of the Certificate of Nationality.
xvi. One copy of the Errors and Omissions Insurance. With coverage for a term of three (3) years from the Distributor's receipt of the Program, naming the Distributor and any other party or parties as the Distributor may designate as insured parties thereupon, such coverage is to have limits of no less than one million dollars ($1,000,000) per occurrence and three million dollars ($3,000,000) in the aggregate, and a deductible not exceeding ten thousand dollars ($10,000)
xvii. List of Unpaid Use Fees – one copy of the list as supplied by the Producer of the Program to the Distributor, at the Distributor's request.
xviii. E-copies of scripts in all/any language.
xix. E-copies of any and all credits
xx. List of Holdbacks.
xxi. Any and all of the underlying rights and chain-of-title documentation with respect to the Program(s).
xxii. Certificate that there are no pending or anticipated claims or litigation in any way pertaining to the Program(s);
xxiii. Any or all financing and deferral arrangements entered into by the Producer with respect to the Program;
xxiv. At the Distributor's request, an opinion from legal counsel that the Producer has all the rights necessary to provide the Distributor with the Granted Rights, and that this Agreement has been duly authorized by the Producer and is sufficient to vest the Granted Rights in the Distributor, free and clear of all encumbrances and adverse claims.
xxv. Artwork

xxvi. Copyright title and credit.
xxvii. Right claim registration authorization letter. At the Distributor's request.
xxviii. Direct link from the movie and the movie Producer's website to the Distributor's website.
xxix. Production Notes: If available, a copy of the production notes of the Series, including items relating where the Series was photographed, anecdotes about the production of the background of the Series.
xxx. A true copy of a CRTC or CAVCO certificate with a Canadian content number, if applicable.

For theatrical Release:

The Picture materials shall be fully cut, titled, and assembled, with the soundtrack printed thereon in perfect synchronization throughout, with the photographic action.
As the Territory includes the United States, a copy of an MPAA rating certificate is required.

2.1 Laboratory Access – Dolby or Ultra Stereo Soundtrack,
(a) One (1) 35mm four-track magnetic master of the final stereo dub;

Physical Delivery – Stereo M&E Track
(b) One (1) 35mm four-track magnetic master, stereo M&E track, with the effects in this dub, fully filled and mixed in the same manner as the four-track magnetic master; and
(c) A copy of an executed license agreement between the Producer and Dolby Laboratories Inc., or Ultra Stereo Labs Inc., as applicable in connection with the Picture.

13. GENERAL PROVISIONS

13.1 This Agreement constitutes the entire understanding of the parties at the date hereof with respect to the subject matter hereof and supersedes all prior agreements, arrangements and understandings between the parties relating thereto, whether oral or in writing. Any amendments or variations thereto must be in writing and signed by duly authorized representatives of the parties hereto. The Schedule to this Agreement is incorporated into and forms part of this Agreement.

13.2 Nothing contained in this Agreement shall be deemed to constitute a partnership between the parties hereto.

13.3 No waiver, express or implied, by one Party of a breach by the other Party of any of the provisions of this Agreement shall operate as a waiver of any preceding or succeeding breach of the same or any other provision of this Agreement.

13.4 This Agreement shall be governed by and construed according to the laws of the Province of Ontario and the federal laws of Canada applicable in that province and the Producer and the Distributor hereby agree to submit to the jurisdiction of the Ontario courts and/or, for matters within its exclusive jurisdiction, the Federal Court of Canada and the decisions of such courts shall be binding on both Parties.

In witness whereof, this Agreement has been duly signed by the Parties.

[Name of Distributor]	[Name of Producer]
By:	By:
Name:	Name:
Title:	Title:
I have authority to bind the corporation.	I have authority to bind the corporation.
COMPANY SEAL	COMPANY SEAL
DATE:	DATE:

ALL PAGES OF THE PRESENT AGREEMENT MUST BE INITIALIZED.

Chapter 12
RIGHTS ACQUISITION

Introduction

The objective of any production is to be sold to as many places, in as many formats and languages, and on as many platforms as possible.

After investing a large amount of money and spending a considerable amount of time on the production of a show in its many stages, the objective is to recoup the investment and generate revenues.

To do that, the show must be sold, but how? Basically, we tend to always think of a broadcaster as the main source of revenue, but depending on what we have produced, we may have to follow a different path. This brings us to a discussion of what we call **windows**.

Windows

Let's not confuse this use of the word "windows" with the popular software package or a part of a house; rather, it refers to the steps followed to obtain the maximum benefits from the sales of the show. It is based on limitations in the size of the audience, going from the minimum to the maximum possible size of audience.

For example, let's assume we have produced a feature film. The first window for trying to sell the movie is theatrical, unless it was a movie created specifically for TV. From there, we will try to sell it to SVOD or subscription-based broadcasting; after that, cable; then free-to-air TV; and finally the Internet. In the past, the production of a DVD used to be the last "window" for sales. But times have changed, and this is not an available option anymore.

As you can see, it makes more sense to follow this structure since, in this way, we can obtain revenues from more sources than just selling it directly to free-to-air television.

The windows system is the standard used by all producers; however, it may change depending on the producer's needs. As an example, these days some famous movies that were on free-to-air television are now back on SVOD. This has happened because, at the time they were produced, the SVOD system was not developed.

There are other cases where a show was specifically produced for one particular medium, such as a broadcaster, etc., and that may create a different starting point for distributing the product.

The Agreement

Below you will find a simple broadcasting sale agreement granting a license to one party to exhibit the production. I say simple as I have had to deal with other contracts that were very long and detailed in my career; these were generally from large broadcasters for large deals. The one presented here is an adequate template for almost any sale as it covers the main aspects of these kinds of deals. In the Basic Terms section, where details of the sale are provided, I have added some explanations of what should be included there.

Please note: This is a sample agreement, and the template must be reviewed very carefully and modified as much as necessary to ensure that it accurately sets out all of the terms and conditions of your agreement. As well, be very careful to check references to the Basic Terms in the Standard Terms and Conditions section to make sure they are correct. Once signed, the agreement will be a legal contract, and each party will be bound by its terms. Legal advice from an experienced lawyer is always recommended before you enter into a contract.

LICENSE AGREEMENT SAMPLE

PART I. STANDARD TERMS & CONDITIONS

1. Licensor's Representations and Warranties

The Licensor hereby represents and warrants that:

(a) It is validly incorporated and in good standing in the jurisdiction of its incorporation;

(b) It has or controls the necessary rights to enter into and perform this Agreement and to license to the Licensee all rights granted hereunder;

(c) To the best of its knowledge, understanding, and belief, at the time of delivery of the Program(s) there will not be any outstanding claims, liens or encumbrances in or to the Program(s) or any part thereof which can or will derogate from the rights herein licensed to the Licensee;

(d) To the best of its knowledge, understanding, and belief, there has not been any grant of license of the Program(s) to any third party contrary to the provisions of this Agreement and that it shall not, during the Term of exclusivity of this Agreement (if any), grant to any other person, firm or corporation any rights exclusively granted to the Licensee except as specifically provided herein;

(e) The performing rights to the music contained in the Program(s) and the right to communicate these rights to the public by telecommunication are either:

(i) controlled by SOCAN or its affiliates;
(ii) controlled by the Licensor to the extent necessary to permit the Licensee to exhibit the Program(s); or
(iii) in the public domain;

and to the best of the Licensor's knowledge, understanding, and belief, all necessary authorizations and clearances for the broadcast of the Program(s) have been acquired or obtained.

2. Representation and Warranty of Licensee

The Licensee hereby represents and warrants that it is validly incorporated and in good standing in the jurisdiction of its incorporation and that it has the full right, power, and authority to enter into and perform this Agreement.

3. Materials

(a) The Licensor shall deliver to the Licensee at the address indicated above or other address designated by the Licensee at the Licensee's expense on the Delivery Date (as specified in Paragraph 1(17) of the Basic Terms):

(i) the Program Masters (as specified in Paragraph 1(14) of the Basic Terms); and
(ii) any stills, press books, and other promotional materials as the Licensor may have in its possession or to which it has access (and which it is permitted to furnish) for the Licensee's use solely in connection with advertising, publicizing or exploiting the Program(s) hereunder ("the Promotional Materials").

(b) The Program Masters delivered to the Licensee hereunder shall be deemed technically acceptable for the exhibition of the Program(s) upon the earlier of the Licensee's notification to the Licensor that such Program Masters are technically satisfactory or seven (7) natural days following delivery to the Licensee. If the Licensee has notified the Licensor that the Program Masters are not technically acceptable within said seven (7) natural days period, the Licensor shall, at its election and sole expense promptly cause such defects to be corrected or new Program Masters to be made and delivered to the Licensee in the manner described in this Paragraph 1(14).

(c) The Program Masters delivered to the Licensee are provided on loan for the period specified in Paragraph 1(10) of the Basic Terms, during which time the Licensee shall make the appropriate broadcast copies of the Program(s) to be used by the Licensee during the Licence Period (the "Broadcast Copies"). The Licensee shall not reproduce, copy or duplicate any Program Materials provided hereunder for any other reason without the express written consent of the Licensor.

(d) The Licensee shall not permit the Program(s) or any part thereof to be reproduced or to come into or remain in possession of anyone other than the Licensee or personnel connected with the broadcasting of the Program(s) licensed hereunder.

(e) The Licensee shall exercise due care in handling, storing, and safeguarding all Program Masters provided hereunder and shall assume all risk for loss, theft, damage, or unauthorized duplication of the Program(s) while in the Licensee's possession, maintaining insurance in sufficient amounts to protect against the same.

(f) The Licensee shall return the Program Masters to the Licensor following the loan period specified in Paragraph 1(10) of the Basic Terms at the address indicated above or to such other place as the Licensor may designate, at the Licensee's expense, in good condition, normal wear and tear expected.

(g) Notwithstanding the Licensee's obligation to return the Program Masters in accordance with Paragraph 1(18) of the Basic Terms and Paragraph 3(f) above, the Licensee shall, within ninety (90) days following the termination of this Agreement:

> (i) return to the Licensor all Promotional Materials and other materials or documents related to the Program(s) in the possession of the Licensee, at the Licensee's sole expense; and
> (ii) erase or destroy all Broadcast Copies or other copies of the Program(s) made by the Licensee.

(h) The Licensee acknowledges that it shall not have obtained any legal title in any of the Program Masters provided hereunder, and the Licensor shall have access thereto at all times.

4. Music Cue Sheets

To the extent required and available, the Licensor shall supply the Licensee with available music cue sheets for each Program(s). The Licensee shall promptly file with the appropriate governmental agency or music rights society in the Territory, a copy of the music cue sheets supplied by the Licensor, and the Licensee shall make all performing rights payments resulting from the exhibition of the Program(s) associated therewith.

5. Publicity and Promotion

The Licensee shall be permitted to advertise, publicize, and promote the Program(s) and the exhibition of the Program(s) on the Program Service from the Licence Period until the end of the Licence Period and, solely for such purposes, to use and allow others to use the following publicity rights:

(i) to use the publicity material delivered through any media (including but not limited to: television, print, radio, the Licensee's Internet Website, etc.), subject to the terms of this Paragraph 5;
(ii) to create and use written summaries and synopses of the Program(s);
(iii) to use the title of the Program(s) and the name, photograph, likeness, voice recording and biography of any person or character rendering services in connection with the Program(s) provided that no such use shall be in a manner that is capable of being interpreted as a direct, indirect or implied endorsement of any good, service, product or institution, other than the Program(s);
(iv) to use excerpts and segments from the Program(s), and to use the sound synchronized with such excerpts and segments separately from the Program(s) on the Program Service and on the Licensee's Internet Website, provided that any segment from a single episode does not exceed one (1) minute in duration and that no more than four (4) minutes of footage is used from the Program(s) collectively; and
(v) to include the Licensee's and the Program Service's name and respective logos and trademarks prior to or following the Program(s)' credits and on all publicity and programming materials indicating the exhibition of the Program(s) on the Licenced Station(s).

Notwithstanding the foregoing, the Licensee shall strictly abide by all relevant restrictions imposed upon the Licensor, of which it is notified in writing.

6. Dubbed Versions

6.1. The Licensee shall have the right to subtitle and/or create language versions of the Program(s) in the authorized Language(s) (the "Dubbed Versions"). The cost of the dubbing and subtitling will be assumed by the Licensee, who will grant free, immediate, and unrestricted access to the Licensor, even if the Licensee has not recouped in full the dubbing or subtitling cost. The delivery of such dubbing and subtitling will be done together with the scripts of the dubbing and/or subtitling immediately after the work is finished and, in any event, no later than one week after the completion of the dubbing/subtitling work via secured FTP protocol on the Licensee's FTP.

(a) Dubbed Versions created shall meet accepted industry quality standards and audio specifications. In creating the Dubbed Versions, the Licensee shall comply fully with Paragraph 7 herein and shall not:

(i) include any other program or other commercial material on any version of the Program(s); or

(ii) do anything in connection with the recording of the Dubbed Versions that could cause the Licensor to be liable for any costs whatsoever, including but not limited to residual payments or damages resulting from the content of said Dubbed Versions.

(c) The Licensee agrees to provide the Licensor access to the Dubbed Versions and, upon request, shall deliver to the Licensor, on loan and at the Licensee's expense, a broadcast-quality master copy of the Dubbed Versions including all opening and closing title sequences, credits, trademarks, and other notices.

7. Alterations

The Licensee shall have the right to make necessary alterations to the Program(s) in order to conform with reasonable broadcast requirements in the Territory, including the addition of commercials, timing and scheduling practices or government regulations, provided such editing shall be kept to a minimum and shall not impair the quality, meaning or integrity of the Program(s) and shall be at the Licensee's sole cost. Except as otherwise provided herein the Program(s) shall be exhibited by the Licensee in its original continuity and in no event shall the Licensee alter or delete the Program(s) title, opening or closing title sequences, credit, trademark, trade name, logo, symbol or copyright notice, unless agreed to in writing by the Licensor.

8. Payment

(a) The Licensee agrees to pay the Licensor the Total Licence Fee in the manner specified herein. All such payments shall be sent to the Licensor without any deduction therefrom whatsoever, provided that in the event that the Licensee country applies any non-resident withholding taxes prescribed by government authorities, then that amount to be retained shall be added to the License fee payable by the Licensee. In the event of any withholding taxes prescribed by government authorities, then the Licensee will provide the Licensor with a withholding taxes certificate. Unless otherwise specified in the Basic Terms herein, all dollar amounts payable by Licensee shall be in the United States of America dollars.

(b) Notwithstanding the Payment Schedule in Paragraph 13 of the Basic Terms herein, if the Licensee has commenced broadcasting the Program(s) prior to the fulfillment of any condition precedent to payment by either party hereto, the License Fee or any installments thereof shall become due and payable as if all conditions precedent had been fulfilled as of the date of the first broadcast.

9. Broadcast Dates.

The Licensee shall provide the Licensor with the broadcast dates of the Program(s) which have taken place pursuant to this Licence within thirty (30) days of the Licensor's written request. Notwithstanding the Licence Period set out in Paragraph 10 of the Basic Terms herein, the last day of the Licence Period shall be the earlier of the Licence Period end date in Paragraph 10 or thirty (30) days following the last broadcast of the Program(s), including repeats, where the Licensee has utilized the total Number of Plays prior to the Licence Period end date.

10. Non-Production.

In the event that the production of the Program(s) had not commenced or been completed at the time of licensing, and that the Program(s) is not completed by the Delivery Date in Paragraph 17 of the Basic Terms, or if for any reason the production of the Program(s) is abandoned or curtailed, the Licensor shall give prompt notice to this effect to the Licensee and the parties agree to negotiate an amendment to the Basic Terms hereof in good faith. In the event that the parties cannot reach an agreement, this License shall be construed as relating to such Program(s) as are produced and available only, and any payment made in advance by the Licensee to the Licensor shall be refunded, on a proportionate basis for those Program(s) that are deliverable. No other compensation shall be payable by the Licensor on account of the Program(s) not being produced or available to the Licensee, and the Licensee shall have no other claim against the Licensor in respect of such Program(s).

11. Default and Termination

(a) Either party shall have the right to terminate this Licence by providing written notice to the other party, upon the occurrence of any of the following events (each an "Event of Default"):

(i) a material breach of any provision of this Agreement by the other party, where the material breach remains uncured thirty (30) days after written notice thereof has been received by the breaching party; or
(ii) the unauthorized assignment or sublicensing of this Agreement; or
(iii) the inability to pay its debts as they fall due; or
(iv) the termination of business, insolvency or an assignment for the benefit of creditors, or any attempt to make arrangements with creditors, or any proceeding under any bankruptcy or insolvency law taken against the other party, where the proceeding is not dismissed within sixty (60) days from the date of filing, or any attempt to effect a voluntary or compulsory liquidation of assets.

(b) An Event of Default by the Licensor is limited to the particular Program(s) to which the default applied. No default as to one Program(s) will be a default respecting any other Program(s), nor will a default by the Licensor as to any one agreement be a default respecting any other agreement. In the event that this Licence is terminated by the Licensee in accordance with the provisions herein, the Total Licence Fee shall be pro-rated in direct relation to the amount of the Licence Period that has elapsed, rounded to the end of the month of termination. If the apportioned Licence Fee exceeds payments made to the Licensor by the Licensee, the difference shall become immediately due and payable to the Licensor by the Licensee; however, if the amounts paid by the Licensee in accordance with Paragraph 12 of the Basic Terms exceed the apportioned License Fee, the Licensor shall promptly return the difference to the Licensee.

(c) In the event of any Event of Default by the Licensee hereunder, the Licensor may, at its option, terminate this Licence forthwith or suspend delivery of additional programs hereunder until such a default has been remedied. The Licensor shall not refund or rebate any amounts whatsoever to the Licensee and may claim all amounts payable (but not theretofore paid by the Licensee) in respect to the Program(s), the Licensor is entitled to retain such amounts by way of partial liquidated damages. Any amounts so recovered shall be in addition to any other right or remedy the Licensor may have against the Licensee at law or in equity.

(d) The Parties agree that any peripheral and incidental reception of transmissions or broadcasts of the Program(s) in territories where such reception is not intended or authorized due to the inherent capability of signals to be received beyond territorial boundaries ("Overspill") shall not be a breach of this Agreement.

12. Royalty Income

All amounts collected by any author's rights organization, performing rights society or governmental agency which are payable to authors, producers or licensees and which arise from royalties, levies, compulsory licenses, cable retransmission income, tax rebates, exhibition surcharges or the like, will as between the Licensor and the Licensee be the sole property of the Licensor. By way of illustration but not limitation, this will apply to such amounts arising from: royalties collected from cable retransmissions of television programs; collections by music performing or mechanical rights societies, blank videotape levies, and any off-air recording schemes. The Licensor has the sole right to apply for and collect all these amounts. If any of them are paid to the Licensee, then the Licensee shall immediately remit them to the Licensor with an appropriate statement identifying the payment.

13. Reserved Rights

All rights not specifically granted to the Licensee herein are expressly reserved to the Licensor ("Reserved Rights"). For greater clarity, rights granted to the Licensee specifically exclude ...., except as otherwise specifically provided herein and all those excluded as described in Paragraph 5 of the Basic Terms. The Licensor may exercise, exploit and/or dispose of any such Reserved Rights throughout the Territory as it sees fit without restriction except as otherwise expressly provided in this Agreement. The Licensee specifically acknowledges that it has not, as a result of this Agreement, acquired an ownership interest in whole or in part in the Program or the copyright therein.

14. Indemnity

(a) The parties hereto hereby agree to defend, indemnify and hold each other (including their affiliates, authorized licensees and employees) harmless from and against any and all claims, actions, suits, costs, liabilities, judgments, losses, obligations, penalties, expenses (including without limitation legal fees and expenses) and damages of any kind or nature imposed upon, incurred by or asserted against the other arising from the failure to abide by any restriction on the exercise of any rights granted herein or for any breach of warranty or representation made herein by the Indemnitor. Each party's liability shall be limited to any direct liability and damage incurred by virtue of the other's breach, as determined by a final order of a court of competent jurisdiction. The indemnities provided hereunder shall in no event include any damages or losses which may be suffered or claim to be suffered by reason of any loss of profits, revenues, or any similar losses or damages, and neither party shall be liable to the other therefor.

(b) The Indemnitee shall provide the Indemnitor with prompt written notice of any claim or action to which this indemnity applies, and the Indemnitor shall be given a reasonable opportunity to defend against said claim or action, at its expense. The Indemnitee shall not settle any such claim or action without the prior written consent of the Indemnitor, whose consent shall not be unreasonably withheld.

15. Force majeure

In the event that the Licensor is unable to deliver, or the Licensee is unable to broadcast the Program(s) due to any Act of God, labour dispute, government regulation, or any other similar or dissimilar reason beyond the control of the parties hereto ("Force Majeure"), the Licence Period shall be extended for a reasonable period of time to allow the Licensee to broadcast the Program(s). Non-performance as a result of any event of Force Majeure shall not be deemed to constitute a breach of this Agreement, and neither party shall be liable to the other for any such non-performance or the costs arising therefrom. When the period of Force Majeure exceeds four (4) months, either party shall be able to terminate this Licence forthwith upon written notice to the other.

16. Notice

Any notice required or given in respect to this Agreement shall be in writing and shall be sufficiently given if delivered personally to the party to whom it is given or sent by facsimile (and confirmed by receipt of transmission), sent by courier or prepaid registered mail (confirmed by acknowledgment of receipt, unless delivery is refused), to the addresses set forth at the front of this Agreement or at such other addresses as shall be specified in a like notice. Each such notice shall be deemed given upon receipt if delivered personally or by courier or registered mail and on the next business day following transmission by facsimile.

17. Assignment

Neither party shall assign this agreement without the prior written consent of the other, whose consent will not be unreasonably withheld. It is acknowledged that an assignment by either party to any corporation that it controls, is controlled by, or shares common control with shall not be deemed an assignment for the purposes contemplated hereunder.

18. Execution by Counterparts

This Agreement may be exchanged by facsimile and executed in one or more counterparts, forming a binding agreement, each of which shall be an original, at such time as the respective signatories hereto have signed and exchanged the counterpart of this Agreement.

19. General

(a) This Agreement:

(i) expresses the entire understanding between the parties relating to the subject matter hereof and may not be modified, renewed, extended, or discharged, except by an agreement in writing signed by both parties hereto;
(ii) shall not be deemed to create any partnership, joint venture, agency or fiduciary relationship between the parties and neither party shall hold itself out as the agent or partner of the other; and

(iii) shall be read with all changes of gender or number required by the context.

(b) This Agreement shall operate separately and independently from any other Agreement as between the Licensor and the Licensee, and none of the Basic Terms contained herein shall serve as a precedent for any subsequent agreements.

(c) The respective warranties and representations made by the parties throughout this Agreement shall survive the expiration or prior termination of the license granted hereunder.

(d) The waiver of any breach of this Agreement must be in writing and shall not be deemed a waiver of any preceding or succeeding breach of the same or any other provision.

(e) If any covenant, provision or restriction contained in this Agreement is determined to be invalid or unenforceable in whole or in part, such invalidity or unenforceability will attach only to such provision or part thereof and shall not affect or impair the validity of any other covenant, provision or restriction which will continue in full force and effect. Paragraph headings used herein are provided for convenience only and do not constitute part of this Agreement.

(f) The terms of this Agreement are confidential, and neither party shall disclose to any other party any provision contained herein without the prior written consent of the other, except as may be required:

    (i) to comply with any law, regulation or order of a court of competent jurisdiction or the requirements of the CRTC or other government authority; and
    (ii) to its financial advisors, auditors, and solicitors, as long as the disclosing party seeks confidential treatment of any such information.

IN WITNESS WHEREOF, this Agreement has been duly executed by the parties.

[Legal Name of Licensor]

By: _____

Name:

Title:
I have authority to bind the corporation.

Date of signing:

[Legal Name of Licensee]

By: _____

Name:

Title:
I have authority to bind the corporation.

Date of signing:

Chapter 13
MERCHANDISING

Introduction

Once we have produced a show, as owners of the IP (intellectual property), we would like to obtain the maximum benefit from it and promote its visibility. **Merchandising** is the development and sale of branded products used to promote an audiovisual show. This is a very popular source of revenue. Royalties are part of merchandising; they are payments made by the Licensee to the Licensor in exchange for the right to use intellectual property such as copyright, trademarks, and patents. "The word 'royalty' comes from the Middle Ages when Kings (royals) had rights because they owned land on which there were minerals. The person who wanted the minerals would pay for the right to take these minerals out of the land."[13]

Merchandising has a strong link with shows and properties that are child-oriented. However, in other cases, merchandising can flow the other way, through **product placement**. For example, we may include a product in our show as a way of advertising the product and to generate interest in it. Alternatively, we may create a show based on a particular object, the first example of which occurred in the early 1980s when Hasbro produced a TV show, *G.I. Joe: A Real American Hero*, based on its G.I. Joe action-figure toy.

On some occasions, what we see is that, even if the product is based on a show, it surpasses expectations and becomes a merchandising brand by itself. There are a series of brands that we can mention as examples. They include some of the most licensed and profitable brands, such as Pokémon, Hello Kitty, Winnie the Pooh, Mickey Mouse and Friends, and *Star Wars*.

Tie-Ins

In our context, a **tie-in** to a work of fiction or another product based on a media property may include recordings, video games, toys, and clothing, etc. The tie-in can be considered as a form of free advertising since it will be exposing the product to a wider market at the same time as it generates revenues.

---

13. "What Are Royalties and How Do They Work?" (https://www.thebalancesmb.com/what-are-royalties-how-they-work-4142673).

Basic Elements of a Merchandising License Agreement

As we have seen in previous chapters of this book, there are some key elements that must be set out in merchandising contracts. The agreement must include everything that has been agreed to between the Licensor and the Licensee because the agreement will supersede any prior discussion between the parties. For our merchandising proposal, the key elements include the following:

- **Identify the properties to be licensed.** This may seem obvious, but it is crucial that we describe exactly what property is being licensed. If it is a trademark, a patent or copyright, the registration number should be stated.
- **Licensed product.** The contract must obtain detailed descriptions of the licensed products, including dimensions, materials, colours, shapes, etc.
- **Grant of rights.** The contract must state whether or not the Licensee is being given exclusivity and set out the agreements about the publicity for the licensed product.
- **Territory.** Which countries are part of the deal?
- **Channels of distribution.** How will the product be distributed and under which umbrella?
- **Term.** For how long are the rights being granted, and are there renewal rights?
- **Approval by the Licensor.** The Licensor must have the right of approval of a model of the product before it is mass-produced in order to verify that the model follows and contains all the elements of the licensed product.
- **First refusal.** The Licensee must have the first right of refusal to any renegotiation or extension of the contract and to produce and license neighbouring or related rights and characters.
- **Best efforts.** The Licensee should agree to use its best efforts to sell and promote the property. It is prudent to try to negotiate a right of termination if the Licensee fails to meet minimum sales targets or to actively promote the product.
- **Advertising commitment.** The Licensee must commit a fixed amount or percentage of annual sales to a common marketing fund.
- **Royalties.** Usually, the Licensee will give an advance to the Licensor and will commit to achieving a minimum volume of sales.
- **Royalty rate** (net receipts from 2 percent to 25 percent, specific by type), and other factors such as whether it is based on the wholesale (rather than retail) price, whether sales are on consignment, any distribution time period (e.g., 90 days) and any base, FOB sales, bonuses, etc. The contract must be very specific about the royalty rate and how it is calculated.

Other factors will include how well the property is known and the distribution charges such as warehouse (50 percent), FOB (fee or freight on board), whether the retailer pays for the transportation from the manufacturer and the respective responsibilities of the Licensor and the Licensee for returns, taxes, shipping costs, discounts (5 percent to 15 percent), etc.

- **Fairs.** The Licensee must guarantee to the Licensor that the properties are going to be present in different events or fairs in order to produce deals for its sales.
- **Point of origin (FOB Origin).** Unless qualified in the FOB clause, the Buyer is responsible for freight charges. The following are the terms used to indicate responsibility for freight charges and their meanings:
  - *FOB Origin Freight Collect*: Buyer pays and bears freight charges.
  - *FOB Origin, Freight Prepaid*: The Seller pays and bears freight charges.
  - *FOB Origin, Freight Prepaid & Add*: The Seller pays and invoices the Buyer for freight charges.
- **Destination (FOB Destination).** Unless qualified in the FOB clause, the Seller is responsible for freight charges.
  - *FOB Destination, Freight Collect*: The Buyer pays and bears the freight charges.
  - *FOB Destination, Freight Prepaid*: The Seller pays and bears the freight charges.
  - *FOB Destination, Freight Collect & Allowed*: The Buyer pays freight charges and deducts the amount from the Seller's invoice.
  - *FOB Destination, Freight Prepaid & Add*: The Seller pays the freight and adds the freight charges to its invoice to the Buyer.
- **Statements and payments.** Sales reports and payments are done quarterly.
- **Audit right.** The Licensor has the right during a specific time period and during normal business hours, to inspect the accounting books of the Licensee. If there is a difference of more than 5 percent, then the Licensee has to pay the cost of the audit and pay the difference to the Licensor.
- **Credits.** The product must have a hang tag or some other marking on the object itself to associate brand recognition with the copyright. Same for the trademark.
- **Insurance.** Merchandising contracts usually have a clause for insurance in case there are any problems with the production, the copyright, etc.
- **Indemnification.** There must be an indemnification clause in case any of the parties to the contract fails to perform its obligations and fails to cure its default within a specified time period.
- **Termination.** The termination identifies the reason for which either party may termi-

nate the contract before the end of the term. The contract may also include a renewal clause setting out the procedure for renewing the contract at the end of the term. Contracts will normally give a party the right to terminate the contract immediately if the other party defaults in its performance of its contractual obligations and fails to cure the default within a specified time period after receiving written notice of the default. In some cases, the termination right will only affect the portion of the contract that is affected by the default.

- **Sales after termination.** Normally the Licensor permits a time period between 90 and 120 days to finalize all the pending deals and liquidate inventory.
- **Withdrawal of a licensed property.** Usually, this happens when there is an Infringement or claim.
- **Legislation.** The contract must be governed by the legislation of a particular country and subject to the jurisdiction of the courts of that country.

Appendix I
The Berne Convention

Berne Convention for the Protection of Literary and Artistic Works
of September 9, 1886,
completed at PARIS on May 4, 1896, revised at BERLIN on November 13, 1908, completed at BERNE on March 20, 1914, revised at ROME on June 2, 1928, at BRUSSELS on June 26, 1948,
at STOCKHOLM on July 14, 1967, and at PARIS on July 24, 1971, and amended on September 28, 1979.

[NOTE: Each Article and the Appendix have been given titles to facilitate their identification. There are no titles in the signed (English) text.]

The countries of the Union, being equally animated by the desire to protect, in as effective and uniform a manner as possible, the rights of authors in their literary and artistic works,

Recognizing the importance of the work of the Revision Conference held at Stockholm in 1967,

Have resolved to revise the Act adopted by the Stockholm Conference, while maintaining without change Articles 1 to 20 and 22 to 26 of that Act.

Consequently, the undersigned Plenipotentiaries, having presented their full powers, recognized as in good and due form, have agreed as follows:

Article 1. Establishment of a Union.
The countries to which this Convention applies constitute a Union for the protection of the rights of authors in their literary and artistic works.

Article 2. Protected Works:
1. "Literary and artistic works"; 2. Possible requirement of fixation; 3. Derivative works;
4. Official texts; 5. Collections; 6. Obligation to protect; beneficiaries of protection;
7. Works of applied art and industrial designs; 8. News

(1) The expression "literary and artistic works" shall include every production in the literary, scientific and artistic domain, whatever may be the mode or form of its expression, such as books, pamphlets and other writings; lectures, addresses, sermons and other works of the same nature; dramatic or dramatico-musical works; choreographic works and entertainments in dumb show; musical compositions with or without words; cinematographic works to which are assimilated works expressed by a process analogous to cinematography; works of drawing, painting, architecture, sculpture, engraving and lithography; photographic works to which are assimilated works expressed by a process analogous to photography; works of applied art; illustrations, maps, plans, sketches and three-dimensional works relative to geography, topography, architecture or science.

(2) It shall, however, be a matter for legislation in the countries of the Union to prescribe that works in general or any specified categories of works shall not be protected unless they have been fixed in some material form.
(3) Translations, adaptations, arrangements of music and other alterations of a literary or artistic work shall be protected as original works without prejudice to the copyright in the original work.

(4) It shall be a matter for legislation in the countries of the Union to determine the protection to be granted to official texts of a legislative, administrative and legal nature, and to official translations of such texts.

(5) Collections of literary or artistic works such as encyclopaedias and anthologies which, by reason of the selection and arrangement of their contents, constitute intellectual creations shall be protected as such, without prejudice to the copyright in each of the works forming part of such collections.

(6) The works mentioned in this Article shall enjoy protection in all countries of the Union. This protection shall operate for the benefit of the author and his successors in title.

(7) Subject to the provisions of Article 7(4) of this Convention, it shall be a matter for legislation in the countries of the Union to determine the extent of the application of their laws to works of applied art and industrial designs and models, as well as the conditions under which such works, designs and models shall be protected. Works protected in the country of origin solely as designs and models shall be entitled in another country of the Union only to such special protection as is granted in that country to designs and models; however, if no such special protection is granted in that country, such works shall be protected as artistic works.
(8) The protection of this Convention shall not apply to news of the day or to miscellaneous facts having the character of mere items of press information.

Article 2bis. Possible Limitation of Protection of Certain Works:
1. Certain speeches; 2. Certain uses of lectures and addresses; 3. Right to make collections of such works
(1) It shall be a matter for legislation in the countries of the Union to exclude, wholly or in part, from the protection provided by the preceding Article political speeches and speeches delivered in the course of legal proceedings.

(2) It shall also be a matter for legislation in the countries of the Union to determine the conditions under which lectures, addresses and other works of the same nature which are delivered in public may be reproduced by the press, broadcast, communicated to the public by wire and made the subject of public communication as envisaged in Article 11*bis*(1) of this Convention, when such use is justified by the informatory purpose.

(3) Nevertheless, the author shall enjoy the exclusive right of making a collection of his works mentioned in the preceding paragraphs.

Article 3. Criteria of Eligibility for Protection:
1. Nationality of author; place of publication of work; 2. Residence of author;
3: "Published" works; 4. "Simultaneously published" works
(1) The protection of this Convention shall apply to:
(a) authors who are nationals of one of the countries of the Union, for their works, whether published or not;
(b) authors who are not nationals of one of the countries of the Union, for their works first published in one of those countries, or simultaneously in a country outside the Union and in a country of the Union.

(2) Authors who are not nationals of one of the countries of the Union but who have their habitual residence in one of them shall, for the purposes of this Convention, be assimilated to nationals of that country.

(3) The expression "published works" means works published with the consent of their authors, whatever may be the means of manufacture of the copies, provided that the availability of such copies has been such as to satisfy the reasonable requirements of the public, having regard to the nature of the work. The performance of a dramatic, dramatico-musical, cinematographic or musical work, the public recitation of a literary work, the communication by wire or the broadcasting of literary or artistic works, the exhibition of a work of art and the construction of a work of architecture shall not constitute publication.

(4) A work shall be considered as having been published simultaneously in several countries if it has been published in two or more countries within thirty days of its first publication.

Article 4. Criteria of Eligibility for Protection of Cinematographic Works, Works of Architecture and Certain Artistic Works
The protection of this Convention shall apply, even if the conditions of Article 3 are not fulfilled, to:
(a) authors of cinematographic works the maker of which has his headquarters or habitual residence in one of the countries of the Union;
(b) authors of works of architecture erected in a country of the Union or of other artistic works incorporated in a building or other structure located in a country of the Union.

Article 5. Rights Guaranteed:
1. and 2. Outside the country of origin; 3. In the country of origin; 4. "Country of origin"
(1) Authors shall enjoy, in respect of works for which they are protected under this Convention, in countries of the Union other than the country of origin, the rights which their respective laws do now or may hereafter grant to their nationals, as well as the rights specially granted by this Convention.

(2) The enjoyment and the exercise of these rights shall not be subject to any formality; such enjoyment and such exercise shall be independent of the existence of protection in the country of origin of the work. Consequently, apart from the provisions of this Convention, the extent of protection, as well as the means of redress afforded to the author to protect his rights, shall be governed exclusively by the laws of the country where protection is claimed.

(3) Protection in the country of origin is governed by domestic law. However, when the author is not a national of the country of origin of the work for which he is protected under this Convention, he shall enjoy in that country the same rights as national authors.

(4) The country of origin shall be considered to be:
(a) in the case of works first published in a country of the Union, that country; in the case of works published simultaneously in several countries of the Union which grant different terms of protection, the country whose legislation grants the shortest term of protection;
(b) in the case of works published simultaneously in a country outside the Union and in a country of the Union, the latter country;
(c) in the case of unpublished works or of works first published in a country outside the Union, without simultaneous

publication in a country of the Union, the country of the Union of which the author is a national, provided that:

(i) when these are cinematographic works the maker of which has his headquarters or his habitual residence in a country of the Union, the country of origin shall be that country, and

(ii) when these are works of architecture erected in a country of the Union or other artistic works incorporated in a building or other structure located in a country of the Union, the country of origin shall be that country.

Article 6. Possible Restriction of Protection in Respect of Certain Works of Nationals of Certain Countries Outside the Union:
1. In the country of the first publication and in other countries; 2. No retroactivity; 3. Notice

(1) Where any country outside the Union fails to protect in an adequate manner the works of authors who are nationals of one of the countries of the Union, the latter country may restrict the protection given to the works of authors who are, at the date of the first publication thereof, nationals of the other country and are not habitually resident in one of the countries of the Union. If the country of first publication avails itself of this right, the other countries of the Union shall not be required to grant to works thus subjected to special treatment a wider protection than that granted to them in the country of first publication.

(2) No restrictions introduced by virtue of the preceding paragraph shall affect the rights which an author may have acquired in respect of a work published in a country of the Union before such restrictions were put into force.

(3) The countries of the Union which restrict the grant of copyright in accordance with this Article shall give notice thereof to the Director General of the World Intellectual Property Organization (hereinafter designated as "the Director General") by a written declaration specifying the countries in regard to which protection is restricted, and the restrictions to which rights of authors who are nationals of those countries are subjected. The Director General shall immediately communicate this declaration to all the countries of the Union.

Article 6bis. Moral Rights:
1. To claim authorship; to object to certain modifications and other derogatory actions;
2. After the author's death; 3. Means of redress

(1) Independently of the author's economic rights, and even after the transfer of the said rights, the author shall have the right to claim authorship of the work and to object to any distortion, mutilation or other modification of, or other derogatory action in relation to, the said work, which would be prejudicial to his honor or reputation.

(2) The rights granted to the author in accordance with the preceding paragraph shall, after his death, be maintained, at least until the expiry of the economic rights, and shall be exercisable by the persons or institutions authorized by the legislation of the country where protection is claimed. However, those countries whose legislation, at the moment of their ratification of or accession to this Act, does not provide for the protection after the death of the author of all the rights set out in the preceding paragraph may provide that some of these rights may, after his death, cease to be maintained.

(3) The means of redress for safeguarding the rights granted by this Article shall be governed by the legislation of the country where protection is claimed.

Article 7. Term of Protection:
1. Generally; 2. For cinematographic works; 3. For anonymous and pseudonymous works;
4. For photographic works and works of applied art; 5. Starting date of computation;
6. Longer terms; 7. Shorter terms; 8. Applicable law; "comparison" of terms

(1) The term of protection granted by this Convention shall be the life of the author and fifty years after his death.

(2) However, in the case of cinematographic works, the countries of the Union may provide that the term of protection shall expire fifty years after the work has been made available to the public with the consent of the author, or, failing such an event within fifty years from the making of such a work, fifty years after the making.

(3) In the case of anonymous or pseudonymous works, the term of protection granted by this Convention shall expire fifty years after the work has been lawfully made available to the public. However, when the pseudonym adopted by the author leaves no doubt as to his identity, the term of protection shall be that provided in paragraph (1). If the author of an anonymous or pseudonymous work discloses his identity during the above-mentioned period, the term of protection applicable shall be that provided in paragraph (1). The countries of the Union shall not be required to protect anonymous or pseudonymous works in respect of which it is reasonable to presume that their author has been dead for fifty years.

(4) It shall be a matter for legislation in the countries of the Union to determine the term of protection of photographic works and that of works of applied art in so far as they are protected as artistic works; however, this term shall last at least until the end of a period of twenty-five years from the making of such a work.

(5) The term of protection subsequent to the death of the author and the terms provided by paragraphs (2), (3) and (4) shall run from the date of death or of the event referred to in those paragraphs, but such terms shall always be deemed to begin on the first of January of the year following the death or such event.

(6) The countries of the Union may grant a term of protection in excess of those provided by the preceding paragraphs.

(7) Those countries of the Union bound by the Rome Act of this Convention which grant, in their national legislation in force at the time of signature of the present Act, shorter terms of protection than those provided for in the preceding paragraphs shall have the right to maintain such terms when ratifying or acceding to the present Act.

(8) In any case, the term shall be governed by the legislation of the country where protection is claimed; however, unless the legislation of that country otherwise provides, the term shall not exceed the term fixed in the country of origin of the work.

Article 7bis. Term of Protection for Works of Joint Authorship
The provisions of the preceding Article shall also apply in the case of a work of joint authorship, provided that the terms measured from the death of the author shall be calculated from the death of the last surviving author.

Article 8. Right of Translation
Authors of literary and artistic works protected by this Convention shall enjoy the exclusive right of making and of authorizing the translation of their works throughout the term of protection of their rights in the original works.

Article 9. Right of Reproduction:
1. Generally; 2. Possible exceptions; 3. Sound and visual recordings

(1) Authors of literary and artistic works protected by this Convention shall have the exclusive right of authorizing the reproduction of these works, in any manner or form.

(2) It shall be a matter for legislation in the countries of the Union to permit the reproduction of such works in certain special cases, provided that such reproduction does not conflict with a normal exploitation of the work and does not unreasonably prejudice the legitimate interests of the author.

(3) Any sound or visual recording shall be considered as a reproduction for the purposes of this Convention.

Article 10. Certain Free Uses of Works:
1. Quotations; 2. Illustrations for teaching; 3. Indication of source and author

(1) It shall be permissible to make quotations from a work which has already been lawfully made available to the public, provided that their making is compatible with fair practice, and their extent does not exceed that justified by the purpose, including quotations from newspaper articles and periodicals in the form of press summaries.

(2) It shall be a matter for legislation in the countries of the Union, and for special agreements existing or to be concluded between them, to permit the utilization, to the extent justified by the purpose, of literary or artistic works by way of illustration in publications, broadcasts or sound or visual recordings for teaching, provided such utilization is compatible with fair practice.

(3) Where use is made of works in accordance with the preceding paragraphs of this Article, mention shall be made of the source, and of the name of the author if it appears thereon.

Article 10bis. Further Possible Free Uses of Works:
1. Of certain articles and broadcast works; 2. Of works seen or heard in connection with current events

(1) It shall be a matter for legislation in the countries of the Union to permit the reproduction by the press, the broadcasting or the communication to the public by wire of articles published in newspapers or periodicals on current economic, political or religious topics, and of broadcast works of the same character, in cases in which the reproduction, broadcasting or such communication thereof is not expressly reserved. Nevertheless, the source must always be clearly indicated; the legal consequences of a breach of this obligation shall be determined by the legislation of the country where protection is claimed.

(2) It shall also be a matter for legislation in the countries of the Union to determine the conditions under which, for the purpose of reporting current events by means of photography, cinematography, broadcasting or communication to the public by wire, literary or artistic works seen or heard in the course of the event may, to the extent justified by the informatory purpose, be reproduced and made available to the public.

Article 11. Certain Rights in Dramatic and Musical Works:
1. Right of public performance and of communication to the public of a performance;
2. In respect of translations

(1) Authors of dramatic, dramatico-musical and musical works shall enjoy the exclusive right of authorizing:
(i) the public performance of their works, including such public performance by any means or process;

(ii) any communication to the public of the performance of their works.

(2) Authors of dramatic or dramatico-musical works shall enjoy, during the full term of their rights in the original works, the same rights with respect to translations thereof.

Article 11bis. Broadcasting and Related Rights:
1. Broadcasting and other wireless communications, public communication of broadcast by wire or rebroadcast, public communication of broadcast by loudspeaker or analogous instruments;
2. Compulsory licenses; 3. Recording; ephemeral recordings

(1) Authors of literary and artistic works shall enjoy the exclusive right of authorizing:
(i) the broadcasting of their works or the communication thereof to the public by any other means of wireless diffusion of signs, sounds or images;
(ii) any communication to the public by wire or by rebroadcasting of the broadcast of the work, when this communication is made by an organization other than the original one;
(iii) the public communication by loudspeaker or any other analogous instrument transmitting, by signs, sounds or images, the broadcast of the work.

(2) It shall be a matter for legislation in the countries of the Union to determine the conditions under which the rights mentioned in the preceding paragraph may be exercised, but these conditions shall apply only in the countries where they have been prescribed. They shall not in any circumstances be prejudicial to the moral rights of the author, nor to his right to obtain equitable remuneration which, in the absence of agreement, shall be fixed by competent authority.

(3) In the absence of any contrary stipulation, permission granted in accordance with paragraph (1) of this Article shall not imply permission to record, by means of instruments recording sounds or images, the work broadcast. It shall, however, be a matter for legislation in the countries of the Union to determine the regulations for ephemeral recordings made by a broadcasting organization by means of its own facilities and used for its own broadcasts. The preservation of these recordings in official archives may, on the ground of their exceptional documentary character, be authorized by such legislation.

Article 11ter. Certain Rights in Literary Works:
1. Right of public recitation and of communication to the public of a recitation; 2. In respect of translations

(1) Authors of literary works shall enjoy the exclusive right of authorizing:
(i) the public recitation of their works, including such public recitation by any means or process;
(ii) any communication to the public of the recitation of their works.

(2) Authors of literary works shall enjoy, during the full term of their rights in the original works, the same rights with respect to translations thereof.

Article 12. Right of Adaptation, Arrangement and Other Alteration
Authors of literary or artistic works shall enjoy the exclusive right of authorizing adaptations, arrangements and other alterations of their works.

Article 13. Possible Limitation of the Right of Recording of Musical Works and Any Words Pertaining Thereto:
1. Compulsory licenses; 2. Transitory measures;
3. Seizure on importation of copies made without the author's permission

(1) Each country of the Union may impose for itself reservations and conditions on the exclusive right granted to the author of a musical work and to the author of any words, the recording of which together with the musical work has already been authorized by the latter, to authorize the sound recording of that musical work, together with such words, if any; but all such reservations and conditions shall apply only in the countries which have imposed them and shall not, in any circumstances, be prejudicial to the rights of these authors to obtain equitable remuneration which, in the absence of agreement, shall be fixed by competent authority.

(2) Recordings of musical works made in a country of the Union in accordance with Article 13(3) of the Conventions signed at Rome on June 2, 1928, and at Brussels on June 26, 1948, may be reproduced in that country without the permission of the author of the musical work until a date two years after that country becomes bound by this Act.

(3) Recordings made in accordance with paragraphs (1) and (2) of this Article and imported without permission from the parties concerned into a country where they are treated as infringing recordings shall be liable to seizure.

Article 14. Cinematographic and Related Rights:
1. Cinematographic adaptation and reproduction; distribution;
public performance and public communication by wire of works thus adapted or reproduced;
2. Adaptation of cinematographic productions; 3. No compulsory licenses

(1) Authors of literary or artistic works shall have the exclusive right of authorizing:
(i) the cinematographic adaptation and reproduction of these works, and the distribution of the works thus adapted or reproduced;
(ii) the public performance and communication to the public by wire of the works thus adapted or reproduced.

(2) The adaptation into any other artistic form of a cinematographic production derived from literary or artistic works shall, without prejudice to the authorization of the author of the cinematographic production, remain subject to the authorization of the authors of the original works.

(3) The provisions of Article 13(1) shall not apply.

Article 14bis. Special Provisions Concerning Cinematographic Works:
1. Assimilation to "original" works; 2. Ownership; limitation of certain rights of certain contributors;
3. Certain other contributors

(1) Without prejudice to the copyright in any work which may have been adapted or reproduced, a cinematographic work shall be protected as an original work. The owner of copyright in a cinematographic work shall enjoy the same rights as the author of an original work, including the rights referred to in the preceding Article.

(2)*(a)* Ownership of copyright in a cinematographic work shall be a matter for legislation in the country where protection is claimed.
(b) However, in the countries of the Union which, by legislation, include among the owners of copyright in a

cinematographic work authors who have brought contributions to the making of the work, such authors, if they have undertaken to bring such contributions, may not, in the absence of any contrary or special stipulation, object to the reproduction, distribution, public performance, communication to the public by wire, broadcasting or any other communication to the public, or to the subtitling or dubbing of texts, of the work.

(c) The question whether or not the form of the undertaking referred to above should, for the application of the preceding subparagraph (b), be in a written agreement or a written act of the same effect shall be a matter for the legislation of the country where the maker of the cinematographic work has his headquarters or habitual residence. However, it shall be a matter for the legislation of the country of the Union where protection is claimed to provide that the said undertaking shall be in a written agreement or a written act of the same effect. The countries whose legislation so provides shall notify the Director General by means of a written declaration, which will be immediately communicated by him to all the other countries of the Union.

(d) By "contrary or special stipulation" is meant any restrictive condition which is relevant to the aforesaid undertaking.

(3) Unless the national legislation provides to the contrary, the provisions of paragraph (2)(b) above shall not be applicable to authors of scenarios, dialogues and musical works created for the making of the cinematographic work, or to the principal director thereof. However, those countries of the Union whose legislation does not contain rules providing for the application of the said paragraph (2)(b) to such director shall notify the Director General by means of a written declaration, which will be immediately communicated by him to all the other countries of the Union.

Article 14ter. "Droit de suite" in Works of Art and Manuscripts:
1. Right to an interest in resales; 2. Applicable law; 3. Procedure

(1) The author, or after his death the persons or institutions authorized by national legislation, shall, with respect to original works of art and original manuscripts of writers and composers, enjoy the inalienable right to an interest in any sale of the work subsequent to the first transfer by the author of the work.

(2) The protection provided by the preceding paragraph may be claimed in a country of the Union only if legislation in the country to which the author belongs so permits, and to the extent permitted by the country where this protection is claimed.

(3) The procedure for collection and the amounts shall be matters for determination by national legislation.

Article 15. Right to Enforce Protected Rights:
1. Where author's name is indicated or where pseudonym leaves no doubt as to author's identity;
2. In the case of cinematographic works; 3. In the case of anonymous and pseudonymous works;
4. In the case of certain unpublished works of unknown authorship

(1) In order that the author of a literary or artistic work protected by this Convention shall, in the absence of proof to the contrary, be regarded as such, and consequently be entitled to institute infringement proceedings in the countries of the Union, it shall be sufficient for his name to appear on the work in the usual manner. This paragraph shall be applicable even if this name is a pseudonym, where the pseudonym adopted by the author leaves no doubt as to his identity.

(2) The person or body corporate whose name appears on a cinematographic work in the usual manner shall, in

the absence of proof to the contrary, be presumed to be the maker of the said work.

(3) In the case of anonymous and pseudonymous works, other than those referred to in paragraph (1) above, the publisher whose name appears on the work shall, in the absence of proof to the contrary, be deemed to represent the author, and in this capacity he shall be entitled to protect and enforce the author›s rights. The provisions of this paragraph shall cease to apply when the author reveals his identity and establishes his claim to authorship of the work.

(4)(a) In the case of unpublished works where the identity of the author is unknown, but where there is every ground to presume that he is a national of a country of the Union, it shall be a matter for legislation in that country to designate the competent authority which shall represent the author and shall be entitled to protect and enforce his rights in the countries of the Union.
(b) Countries of the Union which make such designation under the terms of this provision shall notify the Director General by means of a written declaration giving full information concerning the authority thus designated. The Director General shall at once communicate this declaration to all other countries of the Union.

Article 16. Infringing Copies:
1. Seizure; 2. Seizure on importation; 3. Applicable law
(1) Infringing copies of a work shall be liable to seizure in any country of the Union where the work enjoys legal protection.

(2) The provisions of the preceding paragraph shall also apply to reproductions coming from a country where the work is not protected, or has ceased to be protected.

(3) The seizure shall take place in accordance with the legislation of each country.

Article 17. Possibility of Control of Circulation, Presentation and Exhibition of Works
The provisions of this Convention cannot in any way affect the right of the Government of each country of the Union to permit, to control, or to prohibit, by legislation or regulation, the circulation, presentation, or exhibition of any work or production in regard to which the competent authority may find it necessary to exercise that right.

Article 18. Works Existing on Convention's Entry Into Force:
1. Protectable where protection not yet expired in country of origin;
2. Non-protectable where protection already expired in country where it is claimed;
3. Application of these principles; 4. Special cases
(1) This Convention shall apply to all works which, at the moment of its coming into force, have not yet fallen into the public domain in the country of origin through the expiry of the term of protection.

(2) If, however, through the expiry of the term of protection which was previously granted, a work has fallen into the public domain of the country where protection is claimed, that work shall not be protected anew.

(3) The application of this principle shall be subject to any provisions contained in special conventions to that effect existing or to be concluded between countries of the Union. In the absence of such provisions, the respective countries shall determine, each in so far as it is concerned, the conditions of application of this principle.

(4) The preceding provisions shall also apply in the case of new accessions to the Union and to cases in which protection is extended by the application of Article 7 or by the abandonment of reservations.

Article 19. Protection Greater than Resulting from Convention
The provisions of this Convention shall not preclude the making of a claim to the benefit of any greater protection which may be granted by legislation in a country of the Union.

Article 20. Special Agreements Among Countries of the Union
The Governments of the countries of the Union reserve the right to enter into special agreements among themselves, in so far as such agreements grant to authors more extensive rights than those granted by the Convention, or contain other provisions not contrary to this Convention. The provisions of existing agreements which satisfy these conditions shall remain applicable.

Article 21. Special Provisions Regarding Developing Countries:
1. Reference to Appendix; 2. Appendix part of Act
(1) Special provisions regarding developing countries are included in the Appendix.

(2) Subject to the provisions of Article 28(1)(b), the Appendix forms an integral part of this Act.

Article 22. Assembly:
1. Constitution and composition; 2. Tasks;
3. Quorum, voting, observers; 4. Convocation; 5. Rules of procedure
(1) *(a)* The Union shall have an Assembly consisting of those countries of the Union which are bound by Articles 22 to 26.
(b) The Government of each country shall be represented by one delegate, who may be assisted by alternate delegates, advisors, and experts.
(c) The expenses of each delegation shall be borne by the Government which has appointed it.

(2)*(a)* The Assembly shall:
(i) deal with all matters concerning the maintenance and development of the Union and the implementation of this Convention;
(ii) give directions concerning the preparation for conferences of revision to the International Bureau of Intellectual Property (hereinafter designated as "the International Bureau") referred to in the Convention Establishing the World Intellectual Property Organization (hereinafter designated as "the Organization"), due account being taken of any comments made by those countries of the Union which are not bound by Articles 22 to 26;
(iii) review and approve the reports and activities of the Director General of the Organization concerning the Union, and give him all necessary instructions concerning matters within the competence of the Union;
(iv) elect the members of the Executive Committee of the Assembly;
(v) review and approve the reports and activities of its Executive Committee, and give instructions to such Committee;
(vi) determine the program and adopt the biennial budget of the Union, and approve its final accounts;
(vii) adopt the financial regulations of the Union;
(viii) establish such committees of experts and working groups as may be necessary for the work of the Union;
(ix) determine which countries not members of the Union and which intergovernmental and international non-

governmental organizations shall be admitted to its meetings as observers;

(x) adopt amendments to Articles 22 to 26;

(xi) take any other appropriate action designed to further the objectives of the Union;

(xii) exercise such other functions as are appropriate under this Convention;

(xiii) subject to its acceptance, exercise such rights as are given to it in the Convention establishing the Organization.

(b) With respect to matters which are of interest also to other Unions administered by the Organization, the Assembly shall make its decisions after having heard the advice of the Coordination Committee of the Organization.

(3)*(a)* Each country member of the Assembly shall have one vote.

(b) One-half of the countries members of the Assembly shall constitute a quorum.

(c) Notwithstanding the provisions of subparagraph (b), if, in any session, the number of countries represented is less than one-half but equal to or more than one-third of the countries members of the Assembly, the Assembly may make decisions but, with the exception of decisions concerning its own procedure, all such decisions shall take effect only if the following conditions are fulfilled. The International Bureau shall communicate the said decisions to the countries members of the Assembly which were not represented and shall invite them to express in writing their vote or abstention within a period of three months from the date of the communication. If, at the expiration of this period, the number of countries having thus expressed their vote or abstention attains the number of countries which was lacking for attaining the quorum in the session itself, such decisions shall take effect provided that at the same time the required majority still obtains.

(d) Subject to the provisions of Article 26(2), the decisions of the Assembly shall require two-thirds of the votes cast.

(e) Abstentions shall not be considered as votes.

(f) A delegate may represent, and vote in the name of, one country only.

(g) Countries of the Union not members of the Assembly shall be admitted to its meetings as observers.

(4)*(a)* The Assembly shall meet once in every second calendar year in ordinary session upon convocation by the Director General and, in the absence of exceptional circumstances, during the same period and at the same place as the General Assembly of the Organization.

(b) The Assembly shall meet in extraordinary session upon convocation by the Director General, at the request of the Executive Committee or at the request of one-fourth of the countries members of the Assembly.

(5) The Assembly shall adopt its own rules of procedure.

Article 23. Executive Committee:
1. Constitution; 2. Composition; 3. Number of members; 4. Geographical distribution; special agreements;
5. Term, limits of re-eligibility, rules of election; 6. Tasks;
7. Convocation; 8. Quorum, voting; 9. Observers; 10. Rules of procedure

(1) The Assembly shall have an Executive Committee.

(2)*(a)* The Executive Committee shall consist of countries elected by the Assembly from among countries members of the Assembly. Furthermore, the country on whose territory the Organization has its headquarters shall, subject to the provisions of Article 25(7)(b), have an ex officio seat on the Committee.

(b) The Government of each country member of the Executive Committee shall be represented by one delegate,

who may be assisted by alternate delegates, advisors, and experts.
(c) The expenses of each delegation shall be borne by the Government which has appointed it.

(3) The number of countries members of the Executive Committee shall correspond to one-fourth of the number of countries members of the Assembly. In establishing the number of seats to be filled, remainders after division by four shall be disregarded.

(4) In electing the members of the Executive Committee, the Assembly shall have due regard to an equitable geographical distribution and to the need for countries party to the Special Agreements which might be established in relation with the Union to be among the countries constituting the Executive Committee.

(5)*(a)* Each member of the Executive Committee shall serve from the close of the session of the Assembly which elected it to the close of the next ordinary session of the Assembly.
(b) Members of the Executive Committee may be re-elected, but not more than two-thirds of them.
(c) The Assembly shall establish the details of the rules governing the election and possible re-election of the members of the Executive Committee.

(6)*(a)* The Executive Committee shall:
(i) prepare the draft agenda of the Assembly;
(ii) submit proposals to the Assembly respecting the draft program and biennial budget of the Union prepared by the Director General;
(iii) *[deleted]*
(iv) submit, with appropriate comments, to the Assembly the periodical reports of the Director General and the yearly audit reports on the accounts;
(v) in accordance with the decisions of the Assembly and having regard to circumstances arising between two ordinary sessions of the Assembly, take all necessary measures to ensure the execution of the program of the Union by the Director General;
(vi) perform such other functions as are allocated to it under this Convention.
(b) With respect to matters which are of interest also to other Unions administered by the Organization, the Executive Committee shall make its decisions after having heard the advice of the Coordination Committee of the Organization.

(7)*(a)* The Executive Committee shall meet once a year in ordinary session upon convocation by the Director General, preferably during the same period and at the same place as the Coordination Committee of the Organization.
(b) The Executive Committee shall meet in extraordinary session upon convocation by the Director General, either on his own initiative, or at the request of its Chairman or one-fourth of its members.

(8)*(a)* Each country member of the Executive Committee shall have one vote.
(b) One-half of the members of the Executive Committee shall constitute a quorum.
(c) Decisions shall be made by a simple majority of the votes cast.
(d) Abstentions shall not be considered as votes.
(e) A delegate may represent, and vote in the name of, one country only.

(9) Countries of the Union not members of the Executive Committee shall be admitted to its meetings as observers.

(10) The Executive Committee shall adopt its own rules of procedure.

Article 24. International Bureau:
1. Tasks in general, Director General; 2. General information; 3. Periodical;
4. Information to countries; 5. Studies and services; 6. Participation in meetings;
7. Conferences of revision; 8. Other tasks

(1)*(a)* The administrative tasks with respect to the Union shall be performed by the International Bureau, which is a continuation of the Bureau of the Union united with the Bureau of the Union established by the International Convention for the Protection of Industrial Property.
(b) In particular, the International Bureau shall provide the secretariat of the various organs of the Union.
(c) The Director General of the Organization shall be the chief executive of the Union and shall represent the Union.

(2) The International Bureau shall assemble and publish information concerning the protection of copyright. Each country of the Union shall promptly communicate to the International Bureau all new laws and official texts concerning the protection of copyright.

(3) The International Bureau shall publish a monthly periodical.

(4) The International Bureau shall, on request, furnish information to any country of the Union on matters concerning the protection of copyright.

(5) The International Bureau shall conduct studies, and shall provide services, designed to facilitate the protection of copyright.

(6) The Director General and any staff member designated by him shall participate, without the right to vote, in all meetings of the Assembly, the Executive Committee and any other committee of experts or working group. The Director General, or a staff member designated by him, shall be ex officio secretary of these bodies.

(7)*(a)* The International Bureau shall, in accordance with the directions of the Assembly and in cooperation with the Executive Committee, make the preparations for the conferences of revision of the provisions of the Convention other than Articles 22 to 26.
(b) The International Bureau may consult with intergovernmental and international non-governmental organizations concerning preparations for conferences of revision.
(c) The Director General and persons designated by him shall take part, without the right to vote, in the discussions at these conferences.

(8) The International Bureau shall carry out any other tasks assigned to it.

Article 25. Finances:
1. Budget; 2. Coordination with other Unions; 3. Resources;
4. Contributions; possible extension of previous budget; 5. Fees and charges;
6. Working capital fund; 7. Advances by host Government; 8. Auditing of accounts

(1)*(a)* The Union shall have a budget.

(b) The budget of the Union shall include the income and expenses proper to the Union, its contribution to the budget of expenses common to the Unions, and, where applicable, the sum made available to the budget of the Conference of the Organization.

(c) Expenses not attributable exclusively to the Union but also to one or more other Unions administered by the Organization shall be considered as expenses common to the Unions. The share of the Union in such common expenses shall be in proportion to the interest the Union has in them.

(2) The budget of the Union shall be established with due regard to the requirements of coordination with the budgets of the other Unions administered by the Organization.

(3) The budget of the Union shall be financed from the following sources:
(i) contributions of the countries of the Union;
(ii) fees and charges due for services performed by the International Bureau in relation to the Union;
(iii) sale of, or royalties on, the publications of the International Bureau concerning the Union;
(iv) gifts, bequests, and subventions;
(v) rents, interests, and other miscellaneous income.

(4)*(a)* For the purpose of establishing its contribution towards the budget, each country of the Union shall belong to a class, and shall pay its annual contributions on the basis of a number of units fixed as follows:

Class I 25
Class II 20
Class III 15
Class IV 10
Class V 5
Class VI 3
Class VII 1

(b) Unless it has already done so, each country shall indicate, concurrently with depositing its instrument of ratification or accession, the class to which it wishes to belong. Any country may change class. If it chooses a lower class, the country must announce it to the Assembly at one of its ordinary sessions. Any such change shall take effect at the beginning of the calendar year following the session.

(c) The annual contribution of each country shall be an amount in the same proportion to the total sum to be contributed to the annual budget of the Union by all countries as the number of its units is to the total of the units of all contributing countries.

(d) Contributions shall become due on the first of January of each year.

(e) A country which is in arrears in the payment of its contributions shall have no vote in any of the organs of the Union of which it is a member if the amount of its arrears equals or exceeds the amount of the contributions due from it for the preceding two full years. However, any organ of the Union may allow such a country to continue

to exercise its vote in that organ if, and as long as, it is satisfied that the delay in payment is due to exceptional and unavoidable circumstances.

(f) If the budget is not adopted before the beginning of a new financial period, it shall be at the same level as the budget of the previous year, in accordance with the financial regulations.

(5) The amount of the fees and charges due for services rendered by the International Bureau in relation to the Union shall be established, and shall be reported to the Assembly and the Executive Committee, by the Director General.

(6)*(a)* The Union shall have a working capital fund which shall be constituted by a single payment made by each country of the Union. If the fund becomes insufficient, an increase shall be decided by the Assembly.
(b) The amount of the initial payment of each country to the said fund or of its participation in the increase thereof shall be a proportion of the contribution of that country for the year in which the fund is established or the increase decided.
(c) The proportion and the terms of payment shall be fixed by the Assembly on the proposal of the Director General and after it has heard the advice of the Coordination Committee of the Organization.

(7)*(a)* In the headquarters agreement concluded with the country on the territory of which the Organization has its headquarters, it shall be provided that, whenever the working capital fund is insufficient, such country shall grant advances. The amount of these advances and the conditions on which they are granted shall be the subject of separate agreements, in each case, between such country and the Organization. As long as it remains under the obligation to grant advances, such country shall have an ex officio seat on the Executive Committee.
(b) The country referred to in subparagraph (a) and the Organization shall each have the right to denounce the obligation to grant advances, by written notification. Denunciation shall take effect three years after the end of the year in which it has been notified.

(8) The auditing of the accounts shall be effected by one or more of the countries of the Union or by external auditors, as provided in the financial regulations. They shall be designated, with their agreement, by the Assembly.

Article 26. Amendments:
1. Provisions susceptible of amendment by the Assembly; proposals;
2. Adoption; 3. Entry into force
(1) Proposals for the amendment of Articles 22, 23, 24, 25, and the present Article, may be initiated by any country member of the Assembly, by the Executive Committee, or by the Director General. Such proposals shall be communicated by the Director General to the member countries of the Assembly at least six months in advance of their consideration by the Assembly.

(2) Amendments to the Articles referred to in paragraph (1) shall be adopted by the Assembly. Adoption shall require three-fourths of the votes cast, provided that any amendment of Article 22, and of the present paragraph, shall require four-fifths of the votes cast.

(3) Any amendment to the Articles referred to in paragraph (1) shall enter into force one month after written notifications of acceptance, effected in accordance with their respective constitutional processes, have been received by the Director General from three-fourths of the countries members of the Assembly at the time it

adopted the amendment. Any amendment to the said Articles thus accepted shall bind all the countries which are members of the Assembly at the time the amendment enters into force, or which become members thereof at a subsequent date, provided that any amendment increasing the financial obligations of countries of the Union shall bind only those countries which have notified their acceptance of such amendment.

Article 27. Revision:
1. Objective; 2. Conferences; 3. Adoption
(1) This Convention shall be submitted to revision with a view to the introduction of amendments designed to improve the system of the Union.

(2) For this purpose, conferences shall be held successively in one of the countries of the Union among the delegates of the said countries.

(3) Subject to the provisions of Article 26 which apply to the amendment of Articles 22 to 26, any revision of this Act, including the Appendix, shall require the unanimity of the votes cast.

Article 28. Acceptance and Entry Into Force of Act for Countries of the Union:
1. Ratification, accession; possibility of excluding certain provisions; withdrawal of exclusion;
2. Entry into force of Articles 1 to 21 and Appendix; 3. Entry into force of Articles 22 to 38
(1)*(a)* Any country of the Union which has signed this Act may ratify it, and, if it has not signed it, may accede to it. Instruments of ratification or accession shall be deposited with the Director General.
(b) Any country of the Union may declare in its instrument of ratification or accession that its ratification or accession shall not apply to Articles 1 to 21 and the Appendix, provided that, if such country has previously made a declaration under Article VI(1) of the Appendix, then it may declare in the said instrument only that its ratification or accession shall not apply to Articles 1 to 20.
(c) Any country of the Union which, in accordance with subparagraph (b), has excluded provisions therein referred to from the effects of its ratification or accession may at any later time declare that it extends the effects of its ratification or accession to those provisions. Such declaration shall be deposited with the Director General.

(2)*(a)* Articles 1 to 21 and the Appendix shall enter into force three months after both of the following two conditions are fulfilled:
(i) at least five countries of the Union have ratified or acceded to this Act without making a declaration under paragraph (1)(b),
(ii) France, Spain, the United Kingdom of Great Britain and Northern Ireland, and the United States of America, have become bound by the Universal Copyright Convention as revised at Paris on July 24, 1971.
(b) The entry into force referred to in subparagraph (a) shall apply to those countries of the Union which, at least three months before the said entry into force, have deposited instruments of ratification or accession not containing a declaration under paragraph (1)(b).
(c) With respect to any country of the Union not covered by subparagraph (b) and which ratifies or accedes to this Act without making a declaration under paragraph (1)(b), Articles 1 to 21 and the Appendix shall enter into force three months after the date on which the Director General has notified the deposit of the relevant instrument of ratification or accession, unless a subsequent date has been indicated in the instrument deposited. In the latter case, Articles 1 to 21 and the Appendix shall enter into force with respect to that country on the date thus indicated.
(d) The provisions of subparagraphs (a) to (c) do not affect the application of Article VI of the Appendix.

(3) With respect to any country of the Union which ratifies or accedes to this Act with or without a declaration made under paragraph (1)(b), Articles 22 to 38 shall enter into force three months after the date on which the Director General has notified the deposit of the relevant instrument of ratification or accession, unless a subsequent date has been indicated in the instrument deposited. In the latter case, Articles 22 to 38 shall enter into force with respect to that country on the date thus indicated.

Article 29. Acceptance and Entry Into Force for Countries Outside the Union:
1. Accession; 2. Entry into force
(1) Any country outside the Union may accede to this Act and thereby become party to this Convention and a member of the Union. Instruments of accession shall be deposited with the Director General.

(2)*(a)* Subject to subparagraph (b), this Convention shall enter into force with respect to any country outside the Union three months after the date on which the Director General has notified the deposit of its instrument of accession, unless a subsequent date has been indicated in the instrument deposited. In the latter case, this Convention shall enter into force with respect to that country on the date thus indicated.
(b) If the entry into force according to subparagraph (a) precedes the entry into force of Articles 1 to 21 and the Appendix according to Article 28(2)(a), the said country shall, in the meantime, be bound, instead of by Articles 1 to 21 and the Appendix, by Articles 1 to 20 of the Brussels Act of this Convention.

Article 29bis. Effect of Acceptance of Act for the Purposes of Article 14(2) of the WIPO Convention
Ratification of or accession to this Act by any country not bound by Articles 22 to of the Stockholm Act of this Convention shall, for the sole purposes of Article 14(2) of the Convention establishing the Organization, amount to ratification of or accession to the said Stockholm Act with the limitation set forth in Article 28(1)(b)(i) thereof.

Article 30. Reservations:
1. Limits of possibility of making reservations;
2. Earlier reservations; reservation as to the right of translation; withdrawal of reservation
(1) Subject to the exceptions permitted by paragraph (2) of this Article, by Article 28(1)(b), by Article 33(2), and by the Appendix, ratification or accession shall automatically entail acceptance of all the provisions and admission to all the advantages of this Convention.

(2)*(a)* Any country of the Union ratifying or acceding to this Act may, subject to Article V(2) of the Appendix, retain the benefit of the reservations it has previously formulated on condition that it makes a declaration to that effect at the time of the deposit of its instrument of ratification or accession.
(b) Any country outside the Union may declare, in acceding to this Convention and subject to Article V(2) of the Appendix, that it intends to substitute, temporarily at least, for Article 8 of this Act concerning the right of translation, the provisions of Article 5 of the Union Convention of 1886 [4], as completed at Paris in 1896, on the clear understanding that the said provisions are applicable only to translations into a language in general use in the said country. Subject to Article I(6)(b) of the Appendix, any country has the right to apply, in relation to the right of translation of works whose country of origin is a country availing itself of such a reservation, a protection which is equivalent to the protection granted by the latter country.
(c) Any country may withdraw such reservations at any time by notification addressed to the Director General.

Article 31. Applicability to Certain Territories:
1. Declaration; 2. Withdrawal of declaration; 3. Effective date;
4. Acceptance of factual situations not implied

(1) Any country may declare in its instrument of ratification or accession, or may inform the Director General by written notification at any time thereafter, that this Convention shall be applicable to all or part of those territories, designated in the declaration or notification, for the external relations of which it is responsible.

(2) Any country which has made such a declaration or given such a notification may, at any time, notify the Director General that this Convention shall cease to be applicable to all or part of such territories.

(3)*(a)* Any declaration made under paragraph (1) shall take effect on the same date as the ratification or accession in which it was included, and any notification given under that paragraph shall take effect three months after its notification by the Director General.
(b) Any notification given under paragraph (2) shall take effect twelve months after its receipt by the Director General.

(4) This Article shall in no way be understood as implying the recognition or tacit acceptance by a country of the Union of the factual situation concerning a territory to which this Convention is made applicable by another country of the Union by virtue of a declaration under paragraph (1).

Article 32. Applicability of this Act and of Earlier Acts:
1. As between countries already members of the Union;
2. As between a country becoming a member of the Union and other countries members of the Union;
3. Applicability of the Appendix in Certain Relations

(1) This Act shall, as regards relations between the countries of the Union, and to the extent that it applies, replace the Berne Convention of September 9, 1886, and the subsequent Acts of revision. The Acts previously in force shall continue to be applicable, in their entirety or to the extent that this Act does not replace them by virtue of the preceding sentence, in relations with countries of the Union which do not ratify or accede to this Act.

(2) Countries outside the Union which become party to this Act shall, subject to paragraph (3), apply it with respect to any country of the Union not bound by this Act or which, although bound by this Act, has made a declaration pursuant to Article 28(1)(b). Such countries recognize that the said country of the Union, in its relations with them:
(i) may apply the provisions of the most recent Act by which it is bound, and
(ii) subject to Article I(6) of the Appendix, has the right to adapt the protection to the level provided for by this Act.

(3) Any country which has availed itself of any of the faculties provided for in the Appendix may apply the provisions of the Appendix relating to the faculty or faculties of which it has availed itself in its relations with any other country of the Union which is not bound by this Act, provided that the latter country has accepted the application of the said provisions.

Article 33. Disputes:
1. Jurisdiction of the International Court of Justice;
2. Reservation as to such jurisdiction; 3. Withdrawal of reservation

(1) Any dispute between two or more countries of the Union concerning the interpretation or application of this Convention, not settled by negotiation, may, by any one of the countries concerned, be brought before the International Court of Justice by application in conformity with the Statute of the Court, unless the countries concerned agree on some other method of settlement. The country bringing the dispute before the Court shall inform the International Bureau; the International Bureau shall bring the matter to the attention of the other countries of the Union.

(2) Each country may, at the time it signs this Act or deposits its instrument of ratification or accession, declare that it does not consider itself bound by the provisions of paragraph (1). With regard to any dispute between such country and any other country of the Union, the provisions of paragraph (1) shall not apply.

(3) Any country having made a declaration in accordance with the provisions of paragraph (2) may, at any time, withdraw its declaration by notification addressed to the Director General.

Article 34. Closing of Certain Earlier Provisions:
1. Of earlier Acts; 2. Of the Protocol to the Stockholm Act

(1) Subject to Article 29*bis*, no country may ratify or accede to earlier Acts of this Convention once Articles 1 to 21 and the Appendix have entered into force.

(2) Once Articles 1 to 21 and the Appendix have entered into force, no country may make a declaration under Article 5 of the Protocol Regarding Developing Countries attached to the Stockholm Act.

Article 35. Duration of the Convention; Denunciation:
1. Unlimited duration; 2. Possibility of denunciation;
3. Effective date of denunciation; 4. Moratorium on denunciation

(1) This Convention shall remain in force without limitation as to time.

(2) Any country may denounce this Act by notification addressed to the Director General. Such denunciation shall constitute also denunciation of all earlier Acts and shall affect only the country making it, the Convention remaining in full force and effect as regards the other countries of the Union.

(3) Denunciation shall take effect one year after the day on which the Director General has received the notification.

(4) The right of denunciation provided by this Article shall not be exercised by any country before the expiration of five years from the date upon which it becomes a member of the Union.

Article 36. Application of the Convention:
1. Obligation to adopt the necessary measures; 2. Time from which obligation exists

(1) Any country party to this Convention undertakes to adopt, in accordance with its constitution, the measures necessary to ensure the application of this Convention.

(2) It is understood that, at the time a country becomes bound by this Convention, it will be in a position under its domestic law to give effect to the provisions of this Convention.

Article 37. Final Clauses:
1. Languages of the Act; 2. Signature;
3. Certified copies; 4. Registration; 5. Notifications
(1)*(a)* This Act shall be signed in a single copy in the French and English languages and, subject to paragraph (2), shall be deposited with the Director General.
(b) Official texts shall be established by the Director General, after consultation with the interested Governments, in the Arabic, German, Italian, Portuguese and Spanish languages, and such other languages as the Assembly may designate.
(c) In case of differences of opinion on the interpretation of the various texts, the French text shall prevail.

(2) This Act shall remain open for signature until January 31, 1972. Until that date, the copy referred to in paragraph (1)(a) shall be deposited with the Government of the French Republic.

(3) The Director General shall certify and transmit two copies of the signed text of this Act to the Governments of all countries of the Union and, on request, to the Government of any other country.

(4) The Director General shall register this Act with the Secretariat of the United Nations.

(5) The Director General shall notify the Governments of all countries of the Union of signatures, deposits of instruments of ratification or accession and any declarations included in such instruments or made pursuant to Articles 28(1)(c), 30(2)(a) and (b), and 33(2), entry into force of any provisions of this Act, notifications of denunciation, and notifications pursuant to Articles 30(2)(c), 31(1) and (2), 33(3), and 38(1), as well as the Appendix.

Article 38. Transitory Provisions:
1. Exercise of the "five-year privilege";
2. Bureau of the Union, Director of the Bureau; 3. Succession of Bureau of the Union
(1) Countries of the Union which have not ratified or acceded to this Act and which are not bound by Articles 22 to 26 of the Stockholm Act of this Convention may, until April 26, 1975, exercise, if they so desire, the rights provided under the said Articles as if they were bound by them. Any country desiring to exercise such rights shall give written notification to this effect to the Director General; this notification shall be effective on the date of its receipt. Such countries shall be deemed to be members of the Assembly until the said date.

(2) As long as all the countries of the Union have not become Members of the Organization, the International Bureau of the Organization shall also function as the Bureau of the Union, and the Director General as the Director of the said Bureau.

(3) Once all the countries of the Union have become Members of the Organization, the rights, obligations, and property, of the Bureau of the Union shall devolve on the International Bureau of the Organization.

APPENDIX
SPECIAL PROVISIONS REGARDING DEVELOPING COUNTRIES

Article I. Faculties Open to Developing Countries:
1. Availability of certain faculties; declaration; 2. Duration of effect of declaration;
3. Cessation of developing country status; 4. Existing stocks of copies;
5. Declarations concerning certain territories; 6. Limits of reciprocity

(1) Any country regarded as a developing country in conformity with the established practice of the General Assembly of the United Nations which ratifies or accedes to this Act, of which this Appendix forms an integral part, and which, having regard to its economic situation and its social or cultural needs, does not consider itself immediately in a position to make provision for the protection of all the rights as provided for in this Act, may, by a notification deposited with the Director General at the time of depositing its instrument of ratification or accession or, subject to Article V(1)(c), at any time thereafter, declare that it will avail itself of the faculty provided for in Article II, or of the faculty provided for in Article III, or of both of those faculties. It may, instead of availing itself of the faculty provided for in Article II, make a declaration according to Article V(1)(a).

(2)*(a)* Any declaration under paragraph (1) notified before the expiration of the period of ten years from the entry into force of Articles 1 to 21 and this Appendix according to Article 28(2) shall be effective until the expiration of the said period. Any such declaration may be renewed in whole or in part for periods of ten years each by a notification deposited with the Director General not more than fifteen months and not less than three months before the expiration of the ten-year period then running.

(b) Any declaration under paragraph (1) notified after the expiration of the period of ten years from the entry into force of Articles 1 to 21 and this Appendix according to Article 28(2) shall be effective until the expiration of the ten-year period then running. Any such declaration may be renewed as provided for in the second sentence of subparagraph (a).

(3) Any country of the Union which has ceased to be regarded as a developing country as referred to in paragraph (1) shall no longer be entitled to renew its declaration as provided in paragraph (2), and, whether or not it formally withdraws its declaration, such country shall be precluded from availing itself of the faculties referred to in paragraph (1) from the expiration of the ten-year period then running or from the expiration of a period of three years after it has ceased to be regarded as a developing country, whichever period expires later.

(4) Where, at the time when the declaration made under paragraph (1) or (2) ceases to be effective, there are copies in stock which were made under a license granted by virtue of this Appendix, such copies may continue to be distributed until their stock is exhausted.

(5) Any country which is bound by the provisions of this Act and which has deposited a declaration or a notification in accordance with Article 31(1) with respect to the application of this Act to a particular territory, the situation of which can be regarded as analogous to that of the countries referred to in paragraph (1), may, in respect of such territory, make the declaration referred to in paragraph (1) and the notification of renewal referred to in paragraph (2). As long as such declaration or notification remains in effect, the provisions of this Appendix shall be applicable to the territory in respect of which it was made.

(6)*(a)* The fact that a country avails itself of any of the faculties referred to in paragraph (1) does not permit another country to give less protection to works of which the country of origin is the former country than it is obliged to grant under Articles 1 to 20.

(b) The right to apply reciprocal treatment provided for in Article 30(2)(b), second sentence, shall not, until the date on which the period applicable under Article I(3) expires, be exercised in respect of works the country of origin of which is a country which has made a declaration according to Article V(1)(a).

Article II. Limitations on the Right of Translation:
1. Licenses grantable by competent authority; 2. to 4. Conditions allowing the grant of such licenses;
5. Purposes for which licenses may be granted; 6. Termination of licenses; 7. Works composed mainly of illustrations;
8. Works withdrawn from circulation; 9. Licenses for broadcasting organizations

(1) Any country which has declared that it will avail itself of the faculty provided for in this Article shall be entitled, so far as works published in printed or analogous forms of reproduction are concerned, to substitute for the exclusive right of translation provided for in Article 8 a system of non-exclusive and non-transferable licenses, granted by the competent authority under the following conditions and subject to Article IV.

(2)*(a)* Subject to paragraph (3), if, after the expiration of a period of three years, or of any longer period determined by the national legislation of the said country, commencing on the date of the first publication of the work, a translation of such work has not been published in a language in general use in that country by the owner of the right of translation, or with his authorization, any national of such country may obtain a license to make a translation of the work in the said language and publish the translation in printed or analogous forms of reproduction.
(b) A license under the conditions provided for in this Article may also be granted if all the editions of the translation published in the language concerned are out of print.

(3)*(a)* In the case of translations into a language which is not in general use in one or more developed countries which are members of the Union, a period of one year shall be substituted for the period of three years referred to in paragraph (2)(a).
(b) Any country referred to in paragraph (1) may, with the unanimous agreement of the developed countries which are members of the Union and in which the same language is in general use, substitute, in the case of translations into that language, for the period of three years referred to in paragraph (2)(a) a shorter period as determined by such agreement but not less than one year. However, the provisions of the foregoing sentence shall not apply where the language in question is English, French or Spanish. The Director General shall be notified of any such agreement by the Governments which have concluded it.

(4)*(a)* No license obtainable after three years shall be granted under this Article until a further period of six months has elapsed, and no license obtainable after one year shall be granted under this Article until a further period of nine months has elapsed
(i) from the date on which the applicant complies with the requirements mentioned in Article IV(1), or
(ii) where the identity or the address of the owner of the right of translation is unknown, from the date on which the applicant sends, as provided for in Article IV(2), copies of his application submitted to the authority competent to grant the license.
(b) If, during the said period of six or nine months, a translation in the language in respect of which the application was made is published by the owner of the right of translation or with his authorization, no license under this Article shall be granted.

(5) Any license under this Article shall be granted only for the purpose of teaching, scholarship or research.

(6) If a translation of a work is published by the owner of the right of translation or with his authorization at a price reasonably related to that normally charged in the country for comparable works, any license granted under this Article shall terminate if such translation is in the same language and with substantially the same content as the translation published under the license. Any copies already made before the license terminates may continue to be distributed until their stock is exhausted.

(7) For works which are composed mainly of illustrations, a license to make and publish a translation of the text and to reproduce and publish the illustrations may be granted only if the conditions of Article III are also fulfilled.

(8) No license shall be granted under this Article when the author has withdrawn from circulation all copies of his work.

(9)*(a)* A license to make a translation of a work which has been published in printed or analogous forms of reproduction may also be granted to any broadcasting organization having its headquarters in a country referred to in paragraph (1), upon an application made to the competent authority of that country by the said organization, provided that all of the following conditions are met:
(i) the translation is made from a copy made and acquired in accordance with the laws of the said country;
(ii) the translation is only for use in broadcasts intended exclusively for teaching or for the dissemination of the results of specialized technical or scientific research to experts in a particular profession;
(iii) the translation is used exclusively for the purposes referred to in condition (ii) through broadcasts made lawfully and intended for recipients on the territory of the said country, including broadcasts made through the medium of sound or visual recordings lawfully and exclusively made for the purpose of such broadcasts;
(iv) all uses made of the translation are without any commercial purpose.
(b) Sound or visual recordings of a translation which was made by a broadcasting organization under a license granted by virtue of this paragraph may, for the purposes and subject to the conditions referred to in subparagraph (a) and with the agreement of that organization, also be used by any other broadcasting organization having its headquarters in the country whose competent authority granted the license in question.
(c) Provided that all of the criteria and conditions set out in subparagraph (a) are met, a license may also be granted to a broadcasting organization to translate any text incorporated in an audio-visual fixation where such fixation was itself prepared and published for the sole purpose of being used in connection with systematic instructional activities.
(d) Subject to subparagraphs (a) to (c), the provisions of the preceding paragraphs shall apply to the grant and exercise of any license granted under this paragraph.

Article III. Limitation on the Right of Reproduction:
1. Licenses grantable by competent authority; 2. to 5. Conditions allowing the grant of such licenses;
6. Termination of licenses; 7. Works to which this Article applies
(1) Any country which has declared that it will avail itself of the faculty provided for in this Article shall be entitled to substitute for the exclusive right of reproduction provided for in Article 9 a system of non-exclusive and non-transferable licenses, granted by the competent authority under the following conditions and subject to Article IV.

(2)*(a)* If, in relation to a work to which this Article applies by virtue of paragraph (7), after the expiration of

(i) the relevant period specified in paragraph (3), commencing on the date of first publication of a particular edition of the work, or
(ii) any longer period determined by national legislation of the country referred to in paragraph (1), commencing on the same date, copies of such edition have not been distributed in that country to the general public or in connection with systematic instructional activities, by the owner of the right of reproduction or with his authorization, at a price reasonably related to that normally charged in the country for comparable works, any national of such country may obtain a license to reproduce and publish such edition at that or a lower price for use in connection with systematic instructional activities.
(b) A license to reproduce and publish an edition which has been distributed as described in subparagraph (a) may also be granted under the conditions provided for in this Article if, after the expiration of the applicable period, no authorized copies of that edition have been on sale for a period of six months in the country concerned to the general public or in connection with systematic instructional activities at a price reasonably related to that normally charged in the country for comparable works.

(3) The period referred to in paragraph (2)(a)(i) shall be five years, except that
(i) for works of the natural and physical sciences, including mathematics, and of technology, the period shall be three years;
(ii) for works of fiction, poetry, drama and music, and for art books, the period shall be seven years.

(4)*(a)* No license obtainable after three years shall be granted under this Article until a period of six months has elapsed
(i) from the date on which the applicant complies with the requirements mentioned in Article IV(1), or
(ii) where the identity or the address of the owner of the right of reproduction is unknown, from the date on which the applicant sends, as provided for in Article IV(2), copies of his application submitted to the authority competent to grant the license.
(b) Where licenses are obtainable after other periods and Article IV(2) is applicable, no license shall be granted until a period of three months has elapsed from the date of the dispatch of the copies of the application.
(c) If, during the period of six or three months referred to in subparagraphs (a) and (b), a distribution as described in paragraph (2)(a) has taken place, no license shall be granted under this Article.
(d) No license shall be granted if the author has withdrawn from circulation all copies of the edition for the reproduction and publication of which the license has been applied for.

(5) A license to reproduce and publish a translation of a work shall not be granted under this Article in the following cases:
(i) where the translation was not published by the owner of the right of translation or with his authorization, or
(ii) where the translation is not in a language in general use in the country in which the license is applied for.

(6) If copies of an edition of a work are distributed in the country referred to in paragraph (1) to the general public or in connection with systematic instructional activities, by the owner of the right of reproduction or with his authorization, at a price reasonably related to that normally charged in the country for comparable works, any license granted under this Article shall terminate if such edition is in the same language and with substantially the same content as the edition which was published under the said license. Any copies already made before the license terminates may continue to be distributed until their stock is exhausted.

(7)(*a*) Subject to subparagraph (b), the works to which this Article applies shall be limited to works published in printed or analogous forms of reproduction.

(*b*) This Article shall also apply to the reproduction in audio-visual form of lawfully made audio-visual fixations including any protected works incorporated therein and to the translation of any incorporated text into a language in general use in the country in which the license is applied for, always provided that the audio-visual fixations in question were prepared and published for the sole purpose of being used in connection with systematic instructional activities.

Article IV. Provisions Common to Licenses Under Articles II and III:
1. and 2. Procedure; 3. Indication of author and title of work;
4. Exportation of copies; 5. Notice; 6. Compensation

(1) A license under Article II or Article III may be granted only if the applicant, in accordance with the procedure of the country concerned, establishes either that he has requested, and has been denied, authorization by the owner of the right to make and publish the translation or to reproduce and publish the edition, as the case may be, or that, after due diligence on his part, he was unable to find the owner of the right. At the same time as making the request, the applicant shall inform any national or international information center referred to in paragraph (2).

(2) If the owner of the right cannot be found, the applicant for a license shall send, by registered airmail, copies of his application, submitted to the authority competent to grant the license, to the publisher whose name appears on the work and to any national or international information center which may have been designated, in a notification to that effect deposited with the Director General, by the Government of the country in which the publisher is believed to have his principal place of business.

(3) The name of the author shall be indicated on all copies of the translation or reproduction published under a license granted under Article II or Article III. The title of the work shall appear on all such copies. In the case of a translation, the original title of the work shall appear in any case on all the said copies.

(4)(*a*) No license granted under Article II or Article III shall extend to the export of copies, and any such license shall be valid only for publication of the translation or of the reproduction, as the case may be, in the territory of the country in which it has been applied for.

(*b*) For the purposes of subparagraph (a), the notion of export shall include the sending of copies from any territory to the country which, in respect of that territory, has made a declaration under Article I(5).

(*c*) Where a governmental or other public entity of a country which has granted a license to make a translation under Article II into a language other than English, French or Spanish sends copies of a translation published under such license to another country, such sending of copies shall not, for the purposes of subparagraph (a), be considered to constitute export if all of the following conditions are met:

(i) the recipients are individuals who are nationals of the country whose competent authority has granted the license, or organizations grouping such individuals;

(ii) the copies are to be used only for the purpose of teaching, scholarship or research;

(iii) the sending of the copies and their subsequent distribution to recipients is without any commercial purpose; and

(iv) the country to which the copies have been sent has agreed with the country whose competent authority has granted the license to allow the receipt, or distribution, or both, and the Director General has been notified of the agreement by the Government of the country in which the license has been granted.

(5) All copies published under a license granted by virtue of Article II or Article III shall bear a notice in the appropriate language stating that the copies are available for distribution only in the country or territory to which the said license applies.

(6)*(a)* Due provision shall be made at the national level to ensure
(i) that the license provides, in favour of the owner of the right of translation or of reproduction, as the case may be, for just compensation that is consistent with standards of royalties normally operating on licenses freely negotiated between persons in the two countries concerned, and
(ii) payment and transmittal of the compensation: should national currency regulations intervene, the competent authority shall make all efforts, by the use of international machinery, to ensure transmittal in internationally convertible currency or its equivalent.
(b) Due provision shall be made by national legislation to ensure a correct translation of the work, or an accurate reproduction of the particular edition, as the case may be.

Article V. Alternative Possibility for Limitation of the Right of Translation:
1. Regime provided for under the 1886 and 1896 Acts;
2. No possibility of change to regime under Article II;
3. Time limit for choosing the alternative possibility
(1)*(a)* Any country entitled to make a declaration that it will avail itself of the faculty provided for in Article II may, instead, at the time of ratifying or acceding to this Act:
(i) if it is a country to which Article 30(2)(a) applies, make a declaration under that provision as far as the right of translation is concerned;
(ii) if it is a country to which Article 30(2)(a) does not apply, and even if it is not a country outside the Union, make a declaration as provided for in Article 30(2)(b), first sentence.
(b) In the case of a country which ceases to be regarded as a developing country as referred to in Article I(1), a declaration made according to this paragraph shall be effective until the date on which the period applicable under Article I(3) expires.
(c) Any country which has made a declaration according to this paragraph may not subsequently avail itself of the faculty provided for in Article II even if it withdraws the said declaration.

(2) Subject to paragraph (3), any country which has availed itself of the faculty provided for in Article II may not subsequently make a declaration according to paragraph (1).

(3) Any country which has ceased to be regarded as a developing country as referred to in Article I(1) may, not later than two years prior to the expiration of the period applicable under Article I(3), make a declaration to the effect provided for in Article 30(2)(b), first sentence, notwithstanding the fact that it is not a country outside the Union. Such declaration shall take effect at the date on which the period applicable under Article I(3) expires.

Article VI. Possibilities of applying, or admitting the application of, certain provisions of the Appendix before becoming bound by it:
1. Declaration; 2. Depository and effective date of declaration
(1) Any country of the Union may declare, as from the date of this Act, and at any time before becoming bound by Articles 1 to 21 and this Appendix:
(i) if it is a country which, were it bound by Articles 1 to 21 and this Appendix, would be entitled to avail itself of

the faculties referred to in Article I(1), that it will apply the provisions of Article II or of Article III or of both to works whose country of origin is a country which, pursuant to (ii) below, admits the application of those Articles to such works, or which is bound by Articles 1 to 21 and this Appendix; such declaration may, instead of referring to Article II, refer to Article V;

(ii) that it admits the application of this Appendix to works of which it is the country of origin by countries which have made a declaration under (i) above or a notification under Article I.

(2) Any declaration made under paragraph (1) shall be in writing and shall be deposited with the Director General. The declaration shall become effective from the date of its deposit.

Appendix II
Sample Production Budget
(a) Top Sheet

COMET ENTERTAINMENT INC.
Production Budget - Top Sheet
Movie Title
35mm Feature Film

Acct #	Description	Total
02.00	SCENARIO	
03.00	DEVELOPMENT COSTS	
04.00	PRODUCERS	
05.00	DIRECTOR	
06.00	STARS	
	TOTAL ABOVE THE LINE "A"	-
10.00	CAST	
11.00	EXTRAS	
12.00	PRODUCTION STAFF	
13.00	DESIGN LABOUR	
14.00	CONSTRUCTION LABOUR	
15.00	SET DRESSING LABOUR	
16.00	PROPERTY LABOUR	
17.00	SPECIAL EFFECTS LABOUR	
18.00	ANIMATION	
19.00	WARDROBE LABOUR	
20.00	MAKE-UP/HAIR LABOUR	
22.00	CAMERA LABOUR	
23.00	ELECTRICAL LABOUR	
24.00	GRIP LABOUR	
25.00	PRODUCTION SOUND LABOUR	
26.00	TRANSPORTATION LABOUR	
28.00	PRODUCTION OFFICE EXPENSES	
29.00	STUDIO/BACKLOT EXPENSES	
31.00	SITE EXPENSES	
32.00	UNIT EXPENSES	
33.00	TRAVEL & LIVING	
34.00	VEHICLES	
35.00	CONSTRUCTION MATERIALS	
37.00	SET DRESSING	
38.00	PROPS	
40.00	ANIMALS	
41.00	WARDROBE SUPPLIES	
42.00	MAKE-UP/HAIR SUPPLIES	
44.00	VIDEO REMOTE TECHNICAL FACILITIES	
45.00	CAMERA EQUIPMENT	
46.00	ELECTRICAL EQUIPMENT	
47.00	GRIP EQUIPMENT	
48.00	SOUND EQUIPMENT	
51.00	PRODUCTION LABORATORY	
	TOTAL PRODUCTION "B"	-
60.00	EDITORIAL LABOUR	
61.00	EDITORIAL EQUIPMENT	
63.00	VIDEO POST SOUND	
64.00	POST PRODUCTION LAB	
65.00	FILM POST PRODUCTION SOUND	
66.00	MUSIC	
67.00	TITLES & OPTICALS	
68.00	CLOSED CAPTIONING	
	TOTAL POST PRODUCTION "C"	-
	TOTAL "B" + "C"	-
70.00	UNIT PUBLICITY	
71.00	GENERAL EXPENSES	
72.00	INDIRECT COSTS	
	TOTAL OTHER "D"	-
	TOTAL "A" + "B" + "C" + "D"	-
80.00	**CONTINGENCY**	
81.00	**COMPLETION GUARANTEE**	
	GRAND TOTAL	

(b) Detailed Budget CA$

9/24/2020

COMET ENTERTAINMENT INC.
Production Budget - Top Sheet
Movie Title
35mm Feature Film

Acct #	Description	Total
02.00	SCENARIO	
03.00	DEVELOPMENT COSTS	
04.00	PRODUCERS	
05.00	DIRECTOR	
06.00	STARS	
	TOTAL ABOVE THE LINE "A"	-
10.00	CAST	
11.00	EXTRAS	
12.00	PRODUCTION STAFF	
13.00	DESIGN LABOUR	
14.00	CONSTRUCTION LABOUR	
15.00	SET DRESSING LABOUR	
16.00	PROPERTY LABOUR	
17.00	SPECIAL EFFECTS LABOUR	
18.00	ANIMATION	
19.00	WARDROBE LABOUR	
20.00	MAKE-UP/HAIR LABOUR	
22.00	CAMERA LABOUR	
23.00	ELECTRICAL LABOUR	
24.00	GRIP LABOUR	
25.00	PRODUCTION SOUND LABOUR	
26.00	TRANSPORTATION LABOUR	
28.00	PRODUCTION OFFICE EXPENSES	
29.00	STUDIO/BACKLOT EXPENSES	
31.00	SITE EXPENSES	
32.00	UNIT EXPENSES	
33.00	TRAVEL & LIVING	
34.00	VEHICLES	
35.00	CONSTRUCTION MATERIALS	
37.00	SET DRESSING	
38.00	PROPS	
40.00	ANIMALS	
41.00	WARDROBE SUPPLIES	
42.00	MAKE-UP/HAIR SUPPLIES	
44.00	VIDEO REMOTE TECHNICAL FACILITIES	
45.00	CAMERA EQUIPMENT	
46.00	ELECTRICAL EQUIPMENT	
47.00	GRIP EQUIPMENT	
48.00	SOUND EQUIPMENT	
51.00	PRODUCTION LABORATORY	
	TOTAL PRODUCTION "B"	-

60.00	EDITORIAL LABOUR	
61.00	EDITORIAL EQUIPMENT	
63.00	VIDEO POST SOUND	
64.00	POST PRODUCTION LAB	
65.00	FILM POST PRODUCTION SOUND	
66.00	MUSIC	
67.00	TITLES & OPTICALS	
68.00	CLOSED CAPTIONING	
	TOTAL POST PRODUCTION "C"	-

	TOTAL "B" + "C"	-

70.00	UNIT PUBLICITY	
71,00	GENERAL EXPENSES	
72.00	INDIRECT COSTS	
	TOTAL OTHER "D"	-

	TOTAL "A" + "B" + "C" + "D"	-

80.00	**CONTINGENCY**

81.00	**COMPLETION GUARANTEE**

	GRAND TOTAL

Appendix III
Sample Feature Schedule

Appendix IV
Sample Cue Sheet

TV Broadcast, Radio Broadcast or Theatrical Release

Cue Sheet

Page _____ of _____

PLEASE NOTE: Include ALL music used in your production, regardless of the music source.

Production Company Name:

Performance Detail (please check all categories that apply):

- ☐ Television
  Please list Station or Network: _____
- ☐ Radio
  Please list Station or Network: _____
- ☐ Cinema / Film / Theatrical
- ☐ Foreign Sales (outside the US or Canada)
  Please list Countries : _____

Signature of Producer:

Telephone: _____ Date: _____

Title of Production - Film, Program or Series:

Episode Title and Number:

Date of First Presentation / Air Date:

Foreign Language Title: _____

MUSICAL COMPOSITION TITLE	COMPOSER	COMPOSER SOCIETY (ASCAP, BMI, ETC)	PUBLISHER	PUBLISHER SOCIETY (ASCAP, BMI, ETC)	DURATION OF USE (Min / Sec)	USE Instrumental = I Vocal = V Logo = L Background = B Feature = F Theme = T

Add more pages as needed.

Acknowledgements

With my deepest gratitude to my partner in life; to Beth Moore for her feedback; to my students over the years; to the many professionals who helped me grow; and to my publisher.

About the Author

Raquel Benítez is an award- winning media executive with extensive experience in children's and family entertainment. She has worked in a variety of academic and professional positions in the United States, Canada, Asia, and Europe, with a particular focus on conceiving, creating and developing audiovisual properties and preparing them for the international market. Benítez holds both bachelor's and master's degrees in cinematography, broadcasting and communications from the Complutense University of Madrid, where she is also a doctoral candidate in arts and communications, an MBA from the University of Barcelona, a master's degree in broadcasting and various audiovisual diplomas from other institutions, and a certificate in entertainment law from Osgoode Hall at York University in Toronto. She is a member of the Canadian Picture Pioneers and many international audiovisual organizations, and has served as a curriculum developer, guest speaker and instructor at many colleges and universities, including the Complutense University of Madrid, Louisiana State University, the University of Teesside (UK), the University of the Balearic Islands (Spain), University of Las Palmas de Gran Canaria (Spain), Centennial College, Kennedy College of Technology (Canada), Digital Media Arts School (Canada), the Boss program (Jamaica), Krea8tif (Malaysia), Programa de Aceleracion Naranja (Costa Rica), and the Toronto Film School, among others. She has written a number of software programs and books that are now considered the industry standard, and currently works as a producer and executive producer at Comet Entertainment Inc., where she is also the chief operating officer.